Malaysia

Cultural Awareness and Business Negotiations

Country Study

Contents

INTRODUCTION

In our increasingly interconnected world, understanding and embracing cultural diversity has become essential for both personal and professional success. This series of Cultural Awareness books aims to provide participants with the knowledge, skills, and tools necessary to better understand and navigate various cultural contexts. By investing in cultural awareness, we are not only fostering stronger relationships but also paving the way for more successful business ventures and personal growth.

The expanding Global market presents immense opportunities for businesses. However, these opportunities come with the responsibility of understanding the nuances of various cultures. Unintentional cultural misunderstandings can jeopardise your chances of securing a crucial foothold in this lucrative market. This series highlights the importance of being aware of cultural differences and equips you with the tools to deal with the challenges that may arise when interacting with individuals from different cultural backgrounds.

Individuals and families who have travelled or are planning to move to different countries also face the challenge of adapting to new cultures. Culture shock can be overwhelming if one is not prepared to handle the changes that come with relocating. This course offers practical insights and tools to help individuals and families better understand and navigate the complexities of their new cultural environment.

Cultural awareness goes beyond learning facts or memorizing customs; it is about cultivating a genuine appreciation for the richness of human experiences. This series encourages participants to look beyond their own cultural lens and develop empathy for the perspectives of others. By doing so, we foster a more inclusive and harmonious world where people from diverse backgrounds can come together and create meaningful connections.

Throughout this book, you will be introduced to various cultural frameworks, practices, and traditions, as well as common misconceptions and stereotypes that often contribute to misunderstandings and miscommunications. Engaging with these topics will enable you to recognise cultural differences, appreciate their value, and navigate them effectively.

In conclusion, cultural awareness is essential for anyone aiming to expand their reach in the global market, adapt to new cultural environments, or enrich their lives by embracing the beauty of human diversity. By undertaking this journey, you are taking a significant step toward creating a more inclusive, empathetic, and successful future.

Ask yourself: Can you afford to miss out on the vital opportunities and personal growth that cultural awareness can bring to your life? The time to invest in cultural understanding is now. Welcome to an enlightening and transformative journey.

1. WHAT IS CULTURE?

What is Culture?

The Culture of a people can be understood as the system of shared ideas and meanings, explicit and implicit, which a people use to interpret the world, and which serve to pattern their behaviour.

This includes an understanding of the art, literature, and history of a society, but also less tangible aspects such as attitudes, prejudices, folklore etc. Unconscious or conscious habits are just as important as art and history.

Values - What people say one ought to do or not do? What is considered good or bad - the importance of honesty, or chastity?

Laws - What political authorities have decided people should do, and what the sanctions are?

Rules - What a society has decided its members should do. Social rules about marriage ages, childrearing.

Social Categories- Ways of thinking about people as types. - "friends", "criminals", "lovers", "nobles", "clergy".

Tacit Models - Implicit standards and patterns of behaviour that a person does not think about - knowing how to address a police officer rather than friends. Knowing how to dress for a job interview as opposed to a dance.

Fundamental - Categories and ways of thinking that people take for granted and may not recognise even when pointed out. - thinking in dualities good/bad, male/female.

Culture shapes

- The way we think
- The way we interact
- The way we communicate
- The way we transmit knowledge to the next generation

Culture manifests itself in

- Food
- Religion
- Dress
- Differences in language
- Our expectations of male and female roles
- Non-verbal rules and body language

The first step is in understanding the values and rules for behaviour of our own culture - the "normal" or "right" way of doing things. What makes us different?

Geert Hofstede

Between 1967 and 1973 Geert Hofstede conducted a study on culture across 100 000 employees of IBM in 50 countries. From this he developed a framework to 'measure' the 'value dimensions' of various cultures.

Hofstede identified 4 values which can be related to each culture:

- Individualism
- Masculinity
- Power Distance, and
- Uncertainty Avoidance

Later studies by Trompenaar have added several more; however, I will address the 4 basic values along with one later addition relating to time.

From surveys, Hofstede was able to map the cultures and compare them, and from this extrapolate as to why a culture may act in a particular way.

Taking the basic values separately, measured on a scale of 0 to 100;

	PD	ID	M	UA	LT
MY	100H	26L	50M	36L	41L
AUS	38L	90H	61H	51M	21L
USA	40	91	62	46	26
UK	35	89	66	35	51

H = top third of countries

M = medium

L = bottom third

Power Distance

In this dimension, we explore the concept that not all individuals within societies are equal, reflecting the culture's attitude towards these disparities. Power Distance is defined as the degree to which less powerful members of institutions and organizations within a country anticipate and accept that power is distributed unevenly.

Malaysia ranks exceptionally high in this aspect (with a score of **100**), indicating that its society readily embraces a well-defined hierarchical structure where everyone has a specific role that requires no additional explanation. Organizational hierarchy is perceived as a natural manifestation of inherent inequalities, and centralization is widely favoured. Subordinates anticipate receiving instructions from superiors, and the most desirable leader is a kind-hearted authoritarian. Any opposition to the leadership is generally met with disapproval.

Individualism v. Collectivism

This dimension addresses the level of interdependence that a society maintains among its members, focusing on whether individuals perceive themselves in terms of "I" or "We." In individualistic societies, people are expected to take care of themselves and their immediate family members only. In collectivist societies, individuals belong to 'in-groups' (such as families, clans, or organizations) that provide care and support in exchange for loyalty.

With a score of **26**, Malaysia exemplifies a collectivist society. This is characterized by a deep, enduring commitment to one's group members, whether it be family, extended family, or other close relationships. Loyalty takes precedence over most other societal norms and rules in collectivist cultures. These societies cultivate robust relationships, with everyone assuming responsibility for the well-being of their group members. In such societies, causing offense can lead to shame and loss of face. Employment relationships are viewed in a moral context, akin to a family bond, and hiring and promotion decisions take into consideration an individual's in-group affiliations. Management, in this context, involves overseeing and guiding groups.

To maintain harmony within the in-group, avoid confrontation. In their communication style, a "yes" may not necessarily indicate agreement or acceptance. Causing offense could result in a loss of face, about not feeling shamed in front of their group.

In business dealings, personal relationships are crucial. Building these connections requires time and patience, and it is essential not to openly discuss business matters during initial interactions.

Masculinity v. Femininity

A high score (Masculine) on this dimension signifies that a society is driven by competition, achievement, and success, where success is defined by being the winner or the best in one's field. This value system starts in school and continues throughout organizational life.

A low score (Feminine) on this dimension indicates that the dominant values in society prioritize caring for others and quality of life. In a Feminine society, quality of life is considered a sign of success, and standing out from the crowd is not admired. The fundamental issue here is what motivates people: wanting to be the best (Masculine) or enjoying what they do (Feminine).

With a middle range score of **50**, it really cannot be determined whether Malaysian culture falls either way on this spectrum.

In feminine countries, the focus is on "working to live," where managers seek consensus, and people prioritize equality, solidarity, and quality in their work lives. Conflicts are resolved through compromise and negotiation; with incentives such as free time and flexibility being favoured. The emphasis is on well-being, and status is not flaunted. An effective manager is a supportive one, and decision-making involves participation. In contrast, low masculine countries, which are not feminine enough to be classified as feminine societies, exhibit masculine traits but to a lesser degree.

Uncertainty Avoidance

The Uncertainty Avoidance dimension addresses how societies cope with the fact that the future is always uncertain: should we attempt to control the future or simply let it unfold? The inherent ambiguity in the future creates anxiety, and different cultures have developed various ways to manage this anxiety. The extent to which a culture's members feel threatened by ambiguous or unknown situations and have established beliefs and institutions to mitigate these uncertainties is reflected in their Uncertainty Avoidance score.

With a score of **36** in this dimension, Malaysia demonstrates a low inclination for uncertainty avoidance. Societies with low uncertainty avoidance exhibit a more laid-back attitude where practical experience is valued over rigid principles, and deviations from the norm are more readily accepted. In low uncertainty avoidance cultures, people believe that rules should only exist when necessary, and any ineffective or ambiguous rules should be either modified or discarded. Flexibility in schedules is the norm, and hard work is performed as needed rather than for its own sake. Precision and punctuality are not innate traits, and innovation is generally not perceived as a threat.

Long Term Orientation

With a low score of **41** in this dimension, Malaysia is characterized by a normative culture. In such societies, people are highly concerned with determining the absolute truth and tend to think in normative terms. They display considerable respect for traditions, have a relatively limited inclination to save for the future, and prioritize attaining immediate results.

Acculturation

Acculturation is the process of adapting to a new culture.

- Variables affecting Acculturation
- The amount of time spent in the process – educating yourself
- The quantity and quality of interaction – trying things
- Ethnicity or nation of origin – how far is it removed from our own
- Affinity – willingness to learn and adapt

Stages of Acculturation

- Acceptance of new culture - honeymoon
- Individual starts to feel comfortable in the new culture
- Feelings of anger, hostility, and frustration
- Recovery
- Culture Shock

Generalisations

We should remember that there will probably never be one person within a culture that actually meets these dimensions. Rather this is a tool to anticipate likely reaction of a particular culture. There is never an average person! What should be remembered is that between the extremes, patterns do exist.

The inverse also applies; do not confuse a particular individual's personality as representative of culture. Whilst Australian's are considered sports loving people, there are people who don't like Rugby – as hard as that is to believe!

Stereotyping – setting a standard idea, concept or form. This 'notion' has a deeper meaning to our basic survival instincts.

Bias – a particular tendency or preference, which may prevent unprejudiced consideration of a topic. A 'learned' response.

Prejudice - an unfavourable opinion formed beforehand or without knowledge or reason.

Linear and Circular Thinking

How does culture affect Management?

Our Western (Greek) method of teaching & learning is if there is a problem then I can solve it. We are taught to identify issues as a 'problem' that challenges us. The individual works out a plan and overcomes the problem.

In a culture not rooted in the Western traditions, the issue may not be seen as a 'problem'!! Rather it is a divergence or even a side issue that can be avoided or not confronted until a solution is evident

Managing Across Culture

The management theory of MBI (Mapping – Bridging – Integrating) was developed to understand the differences and work out optimum paths to achieve greater workflows.

2. INTRODUCTION

The Importance of Cultural Awareness for Families and Business

In today's increasingly interconnected world, understanding and embracing different cultures is essential for both personal and professional success. With the advent of globalization and the ease of international travel, families and businesses alike find themselves navigating new cultural landscapes. For those moving to or conducting business in another country, cultivating cultural awareness is crucial to ensure a smooth transition and build lasting relationships in this vibrant country.

For families relocating, cultural awareness is the key to integrating successfully into their new home. By understanding the customs, values, and social norms of a society, families can better adapt to their surroundings and foster meaningful connections with their new neighbours. Familiarizing oneself with the language, local etiquette, and traditions can help ease the challenges of adjusting to a new environment, allowing families to fully immerse themselves in the rich cultural tapestry of a new country.

In the realm of business, cultural awareness is equally important. As countries continue to grow as economic powers, many international companies and entrepreneurs are seizing opportunities in the dynamic markets. Mastering the intricacies of business culture can help professionals negotiate deals effectively, avoid misunderstandings, and forge strong partnerships with their counterparts. By respecting local customs and demonstrating cultural sensitivity, businesspeople can build trust and credibility, essential ingredients for success in any international venture.

This comprehensive guide aims to equip families and professionals with the knowledge and tools necessary to embrace a foreign culture and thrive in their personal and professional lives. Through an exploration of history, values, and social norms, readers will gain valuable insights into the intricacies of a society. Additionally, practical advice on navigating daily life, social interactions, and business negotiations will empower families and professionals alike to make the most of their time in this captivating country.

As you embark on your journey, remember that cultural awareness is an ongoing process, requiring patience, openness, and a willingness to learn. By embracing the unique qualities that make a different culture such a fascinating place to live and work, you can create lasting memories, foster meaningful relationships, and unlock the full potential of your experience in this remarkable country.

The Importance of Understanding Malaysian Culture

Understanding Malaysian culture is crucial for various reasons, particularly for individuals and organizations seeking to engage with the country in personal, professional, or business contexts. Some of the key reasons for understanding Malaysian culture include:

Building strong relationships

As Malaysia is a collectivist society, fostering strong relationships is of paramount importance. Being aware of cultural nuances helps in forming and maintaining bonds with Malaysians, be it in personal or professional settings.

Effective communication

Comprehending the cultural context allows for more effective communication, as it helps in recognizing the appropriate language, gestures, and etiquette to use while interacting with Malaysians.

Navigating hierarchy

With a high preference for hierarchical order, understanding the Malaysian culture will enable individuals to navigate organizational structures and interact with people at various levels effectively.

Managing uncertainty

As Malaysia has a low preference for avoiding uncertainty, being aware of this cultural trait can help in adapting to situations that require flexibility, innovation, and relaxed attitudes towards schedules and punctuality.

Respecting traditions and norms

Understanding the importance of traditions and norms in Malaysian culture will aid in showing respect and appreciation for local customs, which is essential for building trust and rapport with Malaysians.

Business success

For organizations looking to expand or operate in Malaysia, comprehending the cultural context is vital for successful negotiation, collaboration, and decision-making processes.

Cultural adaptation

Gaining insights into Malaysian culture allows individuals to adapt their behaviour and attitudes accordingly, which helps in assimilating into the local environment and avoiding potential misunderstandings or conflicts.

3. UNDERSTANDING MALAYSIAN CULTURE

A Brief History of Malaysia

Malaysia is a Southeast Asian country with a rich and diverse history that has been influenced by various cultures and civilizations over the centuries. Here is a brief overview of Malaysian history:

Prehistoric period

The prehistoric period of Malaysia encompasses the earliest human settlements in the region, dating back to at least 40,000 years ago. This era is marked by the presence of hunter-gatherers and the development of early communities. Evidence of human habitation has been discovered in various parts of Malaysia, such as the Malay Peninsula, Sabah, and Sarawak. The prehistoric period can be divided into three significant phases:

Palaeolithic Period (circa 40,000-10,000 BCE)

The Palaeolithic period, also known as the Old Stone Age, is the earliest phase of human history in Malaysia. During this time, the inhabitants were primarily nomadic hunter-gatherers who relied on stone tools for hunting and food preparation. They lived in small groups and followed the migration patterns of animals, moving through the region's diverse landscapes, including dense rainforests, coastal areas, and mountainous terrains.

Evidence of early human settlements has been found in various locations throughout Malaysia, including the Niah Caves in Sarawak, Kota Tampan in Perak, and Bukit Bunuh in Lenggong. The discovery of the Perak Man, a well-preserved human skeleton dating back to 11,000 years ago, at Lenggong Valley has provided valuable insights into the lives of Palaeolithic inhabitants.

Mesolithic Period (circa 10,000-5,000 BCE)

The Mesolithic period, or the Middle Stone Age, saw significant changes in the lifestyles of the inhabitants of Malaysia. This period witnessed the transition from nomadic hunter-gatherers to settled communities that relied on fishing, hunting, and the collection of wild plant foods. The use of microliths, small stone tools, became prevalent during this era.

The **Hoabinhian** culture, characterized by its unique tool-making techniques, is associated with the Mesolithic period in Southeast Asia. Several sites in Malaysia, such as Gua Cha in Kelantan and Gua Harimau in Perak, have yielded evidence of Hoabinhian tool assemblages.

Neolithic Period (circa 5,000-1,000 BCE)

The Neolithic period, or the New Stone Age, marked a significant shift in the lives of the inhabitants of Malaysia. During this time, the development of agriculture, pottery, and more advanced stone tools led to the emergence of more complex and permanent settlements. The cultivation of rice and other crops, along with the domestication of animals, allowed communities to establish themselves in specific locations and develop trade networks.

Archaeological evidence of the Neolithic period in Malaysia includes the discovery of pottery shards, stone tools, and human remains at various sites, such as the Sungai Batu in Kedah, Pengkalan Bujang in Selangor, and Gua Sireh in Sarawak. The spread of metalworking technologies, such as bronze and iron, signalled the end of the Neolithic period and the beginning of the Metal Age in the region.

Early civilizations

The early civilizations of Malaysia are characterized by the emergence of various Indianised kingdoms that flourished in the region from around the 1st century CE. These ancient kingdoms were heavily influenced by Indian culture, particularly in terms of religion, language, and social structures. The prominent early civilizations in Malaysia include the Kingdom of Langkasuka, the Kingdom of Gangga Negara, and the Kingdom of Kedah, among others. These early states played a crucial role in shaping the cultural, political, and economic landscape of Malaysia.

Kingdom of Langkasuka (circa 2nd - 15th century CE)

The Kingdom of **Langkasuka**, also known as the Kingdom of Ligor, was one of the earliest Indianised states in the Malay Peninsula. It is believed to have been established around the 2nd century CE and lasted until the 15th century CE. Langkasuka was strategically located on the east coast of the Malay Peninsula, which enabled it to control the trade routes between China, India, and the Indonesian archipelago.

The people of Langkasuka practiced Hinduism, as evidenced by the numerous Hindu artifacts and temple ruins found in the region. The kingdom was ruled by a series of Hindu kings, who maintained close diplomatic and trade relations with neighbouring Indianised states, as well as with the Chinese and Arab empires. Langkasuka is also believed to have played a significant role in the spread of Hinduism and Indian culture throughout the Malay Peninsula.

Kingdom of Gangga Negara (circa 2nd - 11th century CE)

The Kingdom of **Gangga Negara** was another early Indianised state in the Malay Peninsula, believed to have been established around the 2nd century CE. Its exact location remains uncertain, but it is thought to have been situated in the modern-day Malaysian state of Perak. Gangga Negara was a thriving centre of trade and commerce, benefiting from its proximity to the rich tin deposits in the region.

The rulers of Gangga Negara were known for their patronage of Hinduism and Indian culture, as evidenced by the various Hindu temples and artifacts found in the area. The kingdom eventually declined and was absorbed by other regional powers, but its legacy can still be observed in the cultural heritage of Malaysia.

Kingdom of Kedah (circa 7th - 18th century CE)

The **Kingdom of Kedah**, also known as the Kedah Tua, was a prominent Indianised state in the northern part of the Malay Peninsula. Established around the 7th century CE, the Kingdom of Kedah was a major centre of trade and commerce, connecting the trade routes between India, China, and Southeast Asia.

Kedah was predominantly Hindu, and its rulers maintained close ties with the Indian subcontinent. The kingdom was later influenced by the spread of Islam, which arrived in the region around the 12th century CE. The influence of Islam gradually transformed the cultural, religious, and political landscape of Kedah, paving the way for the emergence of the Islamic Sultanate of Kedah in the 15th century CE.

The Malacca Sultanate (1400-1511)

The Malacca Sultanate, established in 1400 CE by **Parameswara**, a Hindu prince who later converted to Islam, holds a significant place in the history of Malaysia. The sultanate played a crucial role in the spread of Islam throughout the region and facilitated the development of Malacca as an essential trade centre, connecting the East and the West. The Malacca Sultanate was known for its wealth, cultural diversity, and cosmopolitan atmosphere, making it a prominent player in the geopolitics of Southeast Asia during the 15th century.

Foundation of the Malacca Sultanate

Parameswara, a fugitive prince from the **Kingdom of Singapura** (present-day Singapore), founded the **Malacca Sultanate** after fleeing the island due to an invasion by the **Majapahit Empire**. He established a new settlement at the mouth of the Melaka River, which offered a strategic location for controlling the maritime trade routes between China, India, and the Indonesian archipelago. Parameswara converted to Islam and adopted the title of Sultan Iskandar Shah, marking the beginning of the Islamic era in Malacca.

Economic Prosperity

The Malacca Sultanate's strategic location and its policy of free trade attracted merchants from various regions, including China, India, Persia, Arabia, and the Indonesian archipelago. Malacca became a thriving entrepôt, facilitating the exchange of goods such as silk, porcelain, spices, and precious metals. The sultanate's prosperity also stemmed from the imposition of taxes on trade and the production of goods such as tin and gold.

Malacca's economic success attracted the attention of regional powers, leading to a series of diplomatic alliances and rivalries. The sultanate maintained close relations with China, which provided military support and protection from potential invasions by other regional powers. The Chinese admiral Zheng He, famous for his maritime expeditions, visited Malacca several times, further strengthening the ties between the two states.

Cultural Diversity and Administration

The Malacca Sultanate was a melting pot of different cultures and religions, including Malays, Chinese, Indians, Arabs, and Persians. The cosmopolitan atmosphere of the sultanate facilitated cultural exchange and fostered a climate of religious tolerance. Despite the predominance of Islam, other religious traditions such as Hinduism, Buddhism, and Christianity continued to be practiced within the sultanate.

The administration of the Malacca Sultanate was centralized, with the sultan holding absolute authority. He was supported by a group of ministers who were responsible for various aspects of governance, such as finance, defence, and religious affairs. The legal system was based on Islamic law, which was supplemented by traditional Malay customs and regulations.

Decline and Fall

The Malacca Sultanate's prosperity and strategic location attracted the interest of European powers, particularly the Portuguese, who were looking to establish a foothold in the lucrative spice trade. In 1511, under the command of **Afonso de Albuquerque**, the Portuguese launched an attack on Malacca and successfully captured the city. The fall of the Malacca Sultanate marked the end of its dominance in the region and the beginning of European colonial influence in Malaysia.

Colonial period

The colonial period in Malaysia spans from the early 16th century to the mid-20th century, during which the region experienced successive waves of European colonization. The Portuguese, Dutch, and British all established a presence in Malaysia, leaving indelible marks on the nation's culture, economy, and political landscape. This era witnessed significant changes in Malaysia's socio-political dynamics, which laid the foundation for its modern identity.

Portuguese Rule (1511-1641)

The Portuguese, driven by their desire to dominate the spice trade, were the first European power to establish a presence in Malaysia. In 1511, they captured the city of Malacca, marking the end of the Malacca Sultanate's rule. Under Portuguese control, Malacca continued to serve as a vital trading hub, but its prominence declined as competing ports emerged in the region.

During their 130-year rule, the Portuguese constructed the **A Famosa fortress**, which served as a symbol of their authority. They also attempted to convert the local population to Christianity, which met with limited success. The Portuguese era in Malaysia came to an end in 1641 when the **Dutch East India Company** (VOC) captured Malacca.

Dutch Rule (1641-1824)

The Dutch sought to secure their monopoly on the spice trade by capturing Malacca, which they accomplished in 1641. Under Dutch rule, Malacca's status as a trading centre further diminished, as the Dutch shifted the focus of regional trade to their stronghold in Batavia (present-day Jakarta).

Despite their economic interests, the Dutch did not impose significant cultural or religious changes on the local population. They maintained a relatively hands-off approach to governance, focusing primarily on trade and enforcing Dutch monopoly over the spice trade. However, they did introduce new agricultural practices, such as the cultivation of cash crops like coffee, sugar, and tobacco.

British colonial era

The British colonial period in Malaysia spanned from 1824 to 1957, during which the nation underwent significant transformations in its political, economic, and social spheres. The **British East India Company** initially established control over Malacca, gradually expanding its influence over the Malay Peninsula through a combination of direct rule and protectorates. This period laid the foundation for Malaysia's modern identity and shaped its path towards independence.

British Expansion in the Malay Peninsula

In 1824, the Anglo-Dutch Treaty led to the transfer of Malacca to the British East India Company, marking the beginning of British rule in Malaysia. The British expanded their influence in the region by establishing protectorates over several Malay states, including Penang, Singapore, and Malacca, which formed the Straits Settlements in 1826. The British sphere of influence continued to grow, culminating in the formation of the **Federated Malay States** in 1895 and the **Unfederated Malay States** in the early 20th century.

Economic Reforms and Infrastructure Development

The British introduced a range of economic reforms in Malaysia, focusing on the exploitation of the region's natural resources. Tin mining and rubber cultivation emerged as major industries, transforming the country's economic landscape. The British developed an extensive infrastructure network, including railways, roads, and ports, to facilitate trade and transportation.

In addition to the extraction of natural resources, the British established plantations for the cultivation of cash crops such as tea, coffee, and tobacco. The demand for labour in these industries led to the large-scale migration of Chinese and Indian workers, which contributed to the diversification of Malaysia's population and the development of its multicultural society.

Administrative Reforms

The British implemented several administrative reforms in Malaysia, dividing the region into two main categories: The Federated Malay States, which were governed directly by **British Residents**, and the Unfederated Malay States, where British Advisors held significant influence but allowed local rulers to retain nominal authority.

The British introduced a more centralized and efficient administrative system, streamlining the bureaucracy and modernizing the legal framework. English became the official language of administration and education, leading to the establishment of English-medium schools and the promotion of Western-style education.

Social Impact and Emergence of Nationalism

The British colonial period had a significant social impact on Malaysia. The introduction of English as the medium of instruction and the promotion of Western-style education led to the emergence of a new class of educated Malays, who became instrumental in the push for independence.

The colonial policies of divide and rule, which sought to maintain control by emphasizing ethnic and religious differences, inadvertently fostered the growth of nationalist sentiments. Various nationalist movements began to emerge, such as the **Kesatuan Melayu Muda** (Young Malays Union) and the **Malayan Communist Party**, which sought to challenge British rule and work towards independence.

World War II and Japanese Occupation (1941-1945)

World War II had a profound impact on Malaysia, particularly during the Japanese occupation from 1941 to 1945. This turbulent period in the country's history was marked by widespread suffering, resistance movements, and a shift in the balance of power in the region. The occupation disrupted the social, political, and economic order in Malaysia, setting the stage for the post-war struggle for independence.

Japanese Invasion and Occupation

The Japanese invasion of Malaysia began in December 1941, when Japanese forces landed in Kota Bharu, on the east coast of the Malay Peninsula. The British colonial forces, ill-prepared for the Japanese onslaught, were quickly overwhelmed. By January 1942, the Japanese had captured the key cities of Penang, Kuala Lumpur, and Singapore, effectively gaining control over the entire Malay Peninsula.

The Japanese occupation of Malaysia was characterized by harsh rule and a strict military administration. The occupiers aimed to establish a "Greater East Asia Co-Prosperity Sphere," which sought to promote cooperation and unity among Asian nations under Japanese leadership. However, in practice, this meant that the Japanese prioritized their own interests and exploited the resources of the occupied territories.

Economic Hardship and Suffering

The Japanese occupation brought immense suffering and hardship to the people of Malaysia. The economy was severely disrupted, as the Japanese requisitioned resources, such as rubber and tin, for their war effort. The local currency was replaced with the Japanese-issued "banana money," which rapidly lost its value and led to rampant inflation.

The occupiers imposed strict rationing, leading to widespread food shortages and malnutrition. Forced labour, known as "romusha," was implemented, with thousands of Malaysians conscripted to work on projects such as the infamous Burma Railway. Many suffered from abuse, poor living conditions, and a lack of medical care, leading to a high death rate among the forced labourers.

Resistance Movements

Despite the harsh conditions, various resistance movements emerged during the Japanese occupation. The Malayan Peoples' Anti-Japanese Army (MPAJA), a guerrilla force primarily composed of Chinese Malaysians and supported by the British, carried out sabotage and ambushes against the Japanese forces. The MPAJA later formed the basis for the Malayan Communist Party's military wing during the Malayan Emergency.

The Malay resistance, although less organized, also played a significant role in opposing the Japanese occupation. Many Malays resented the Japanese for disrupting their traditional way of life and undermining the authority of the Malay rulers. Some local leaders, such as Panglima Salleh of Pahang, organized their followers to resist the Japanese through hit-and-run tactics and intelligence-gathering.

End of Occupation and Aftermath

The tide of World War II began to turn against Japan in 1944, and by August 1945, following the atomic bombings of Hiroshima and Nagasaki, Japan announced its surrender. British forces returned to Malaysia in September 1945, marking the end of the Japanese occupation.

The experience of the Japanese occupation had a lasting impact on Malaysia. It exposed the weaknesses of British colonial rule and fostered a sense of nationalism among the population. The resistance movements that had formed during the occupation laid the groundwork for future political struggles, contributing to the eventual push for independence.

Road to independence

The road to Malaysian independence was a complex and challenging journey, marked by political struggles, social changes, and the emergence of various nationalist movements. The path to independence was shaped by the nation's experiences during the British colonial period, World War II, and the Japanese occupation. It was during these years that the foundations for Malaysia's eventual independence were laid, culminating in the formation of a sovereign and democratic nation in 1957.

Post-War Struggles and the Emergence of Nationalism

After the end of World War II and the Japanese occupation, the British returned to Malaysia, intending to reassert their authority. However, the war had significantly weakened the British Empire, and the local population was increasingly resistant to colonial rule. The experience of the occupation had awakened a sense of nationalism and self-determination among the people of Malaysia.

Several nationalist movements began to emerge in the post-war years, such as the **Kesatuan Melayu Muda** (Young Malays Union) and the **Malayan Communist Party**. These organizations sought to challenge British rule and work towards self-governance for Malaysia.

The Malayan Union Proposal and the Formation of UMNO

In 1946, the British proposed the formation of the **Malayan Union**, which sought to centralize administration and grant equal citizenship rights to all residents of the Malay Peninsula, regardless of ethnicity. However, the proposal was met with strong opposition from the Malays, who feared that their political, economic, and social standing would be threatened.

In response to the Malayan Union proposal, the **United Malays National Organisation** (UMNO) was formed. UMNO emerged as the leading political force advocating for Malay rights and self-governance. It played a crucial role in uniting the Malays against the Malayan Union and, eventually, in the push for independence.

The Federation of Malaya and the Alliance Party

Following the failure of the Malayan Union, the British agreed to the formation of the **Federation of Malaya** in 1948. This new political entity granted greater autonomy to the Malay states and established a more balanced power-sharing arrangement between the Malays and the non-Malay communities.

The **Alliance Party**, a coalition of UMNO, the **Malayan Chinese Association** (MCA), and the **Malayan Indian Congress** (MIC), was formed in 1952. The Alliance Party sought to represent the interests of all major ethnic groups in Malaysia and played a pivotal role in the nation's journey towards independence.

Negotiations for Independence and the 1955 General Elections

In the early 1950s, the British government began to recognize the inevitability of Malayan independence. Negotiations commenced between the British authorities and the Alliance Party, with the aim of establishing a roadmap for self-governance.

In 1955, the first general elections were held in the Federation of Malaya. The Alliance Party won a landslide victory, capturing 51 out of the 52 seats contested. This decisive electoral outcome demonstrated the overwhelming popular support for the Alliance Party's vision of an independent Malaysia.

Malaysian Independence and the Birth of a Nation

Following the 1955 elections, the Alliance Party continued negotiations with the British government. On August 31, 1957, the Federation of Malaya achieved its independence, marking the end of British colonial rule. **Tunku Abdul Rahman**, the leader of UMNO and the Alliance Party, became the first Prime Minister of independent Malaysia.

Formation of Malaysia

The formation of Malaysia was a significant milestone in the nation's history, marking the culmination of a complex process of political negotiations, territorial expansion, and the merging of diverse cultures and traditions. On September 16, 1963, the Federation of Malaya, Singapore, North Borneo (now Sabah), and Sarawak joined together to form the new nation of Malaysia. This union represented the aspirations of the people of the region for greater unity, prosperity, and self-determination.

Background: The Federation of Malaya and the Borneo Territories

The Federation of Malaya, established in 1948, gained independence from the British in 1957. The nation was predominantly Malay and had a strong system of governance under the leadership of the United Malays National Organisation (UMNO) and the Alliance Party. Meanwhile, the Borneo territories of North Borneo and Sarawak, along with the island nation of Singapore, remained under British colonial rule.

Throughout the late 1950s and early 1960s, the idea of merging the Federation of Malaya with the British colonies of Singapore, North Borneo, and Sarawak began to gain momentum. Several factors contributed to the push for the formation of Malaysia, including the desire to create a larger and more diverse nation, which would promote regional stability, economic growth, and social integration.

Cobbold Commission and the Malaysia Agreement

In 1961, the Prime Minister of the Federation of Malaya, Tunku Abdul Rahman, proposed the formation of Malaysia. The British government, recognizing the potential benefits of a larger, unified nation, agreed to consider the proposal. To assess the viability of the proposed union, the British formed the **Cobbold Commission** in 1962. The commission was tasked with gauging the opinions of the people of North Borneo and Sarawak on the proposed merger.

The Cobbold Commission found that a majority of the people in the Borneo territories supported the idea of joining the Federation of Malaya, provided that their rights and interests were protected. Following the commission's recommendations, the leaders of the Federation of Malaya, Singapore, North Borneo, and Sarawak met in London in 1963 to negotiate the terms of the merger. **The Malaysia Agreement** was signed on July 9, 1963, setting the stage for the formation of the new nation.

The Formation of Malaysia and its Challenges

On September 16, 1963, Malaysia was officially formed, with the Federation of Malaya, Singapore, North Borneo, and Sarawak coming together as a single nation. The new country was a diverse and multicultural entity, comprising a wide range of ethnic groups, religions, and languages.

However, the formation of Malaysia was not without its challenges. The new nation faced political tensions between the central government and the states, as well as between the various ethnic and religious communities. One of the most significant challenges was the relationship between the predominantly Malay federal government and the Chinese-majority Singapore, which ultimately led to Singapore's expulsion from Malaysia in 1965.

The new nation also faced external threats, most notably the **Indonesian Confrontation** (1963-1966). Indonesia, under the leadership of President Sukarno, opposed the formation of Malaysia and launched a campaign of armed conflict and diplomatic pressure against the new nation. However, Malaysia, with the support of the British and Commonwealth forces, successfully resisted the Indonesian challenge and emerged as a stable and prosperous country.

Modern Malaysia

Modern Malaysia is a vibrant and dynamic nation that has come a long way since its formation in 1963. The country has made remarkable progress in various areas, including economic development, social integration, and political stability. Today, Malaysia is a thriving multicultural society that stands as a testament to the resilience and determination of its people. This growth and progress can be attributed to several factors, including a diverse economy, political reforms, and the promotion of national unity.

Economic Development

One of the most significant aspects of modern Malaysia is its impressive economic growth. Since the 1970s, the country has transformed itself from a predominantly agricultural and resource-based economy into a diversified and industrialized nation. Key sectors of the Malaysian economy include electronics, palm oil, petroleum, tourism, and manufacturing. This economic diversification has contributed to the nation's steady growth and has helped to reduce poverty levels significantly.

The Malaysian government has implemented various policies and initiatives to encourage economic growth, such as the New Economic Policy (1971-1990) and the Economic Transformation Programme (2010-2020). These programs have aimed to promote industrialization, attract foreign investment, and develop human capital. As a result, Malaysia has become one of Southeast Asia's leading economies and is on track to achieve high-income status in the coming years.

Political Reforms

Modern Malaysia has also seen significant political reforms, particularly in recent years. While the country has been dominated by the ruling coalition of the United Malays National Organisation (UMNO) and the Barisan Nasional (BN) for much of its history, the political landscape has become increasingly competitive and diverse.

In the 2018 general elections, the opposition coalition Pakatan Harapan (PH) achieved a historic victory, ending the BN's 61-year rule. This electoral outcome marked a significant turning point in Malaysian politics, signalling a growing appetite for change and reform among the population. Since then, the country has witnessed greater political openness, with an emphasis on transparency, accountability, and the rule of law.

The Promotion of National Unity

One of the defining characteristics of modern Malaysia is its multicultural and multiethnic society. The country is home to a diverse population comprising Malays, Chinese, Indians, and numerous indigenous groups. This diversity has historically presented challenges in terms of social integration and national unity.

However, successive Malaysian governments have made concerted efforts to promote national unity and social cohesion. Initiatives such as the Rukun Negara (National Principles) and the 1Malaysia campaign have sought to encourage mutual respect, understanding, and cooperation among the different ethnic and religious communities. These efforts have contributed to the development of a shared national identity and a more inclusive society.

Challenges and the Path Forward

Despite its many achievements, modern Malaysia continues to face challenges. Key issues include income inequality, corruption, environmental concerns, and political polarization. To address these challenges, the country will need to pursue further reforms, strengthen its democratic institutions, and promote greater social inclusion.

Religion, Values, and Social Norms

Malaysia is a diverse and multicultural nation, where various ethnic groups coexist harmoniously. This diversity is reflected in the country's religious practices, values, and social norms, which are deeply intertwined with the nation's historical and cultural heritage. In Malaysia, the main religions are Islam, Buddhism, Hinduism, and Christianity, with Islam being the official religion. This rich tapestry of beliefs and customs shapes the fabric of Malaysian society and contributes to the nation's unique identity.

Religion

Islam is the predominant religion in Malaysia, with approximately 61% of the population adhering to the faith. The majority of Malaysian Muslims are ethnic Malays, and Islam plays a central role in their culture and identity. Islamic principles and values influence various aspects of Malaysian life, including family structures, education, and the legal system. Malaysia practices a moderate form of Islam that promotes tolerance and understanding between different religious groups.

Besides Islam, other religions practiced in Malaysia include Buddhism (approximately 20% of the population), Christianity (9%), and Hinduism (6%). These faiths are primarily associated with the nation's Chinese, Indian, and indigenous communities. Religious freedom is constitutionally guaranteed in Malaysia, and people from different faiths coexist peacefully and engage in interfaith dialogue.

Values

Malaysian society is characterized by a set of core values that reflect the nation's diverse cultural and religious heritage. Some of these values include:

Respect for elders

Malaysians place great importance on showing respect and deference to older individuals. This is evident in social interactions, where younger people are expected to address elders using honorific titles and display politeness in their behaviour.

Harmony and tolerance

Given Malaysia's multicultural and multi-religious context, the value of living harmoniously and tolerating differences is paramount. Malaysians often emphasize the importance of avoiding conflict and maintaining social harmony, even when disagreements arise.

Collectivism and family orientation

Malaysians have a strong sense of collective identity and prioritize family ties. Extended family networks play a crucial role in providing emotional and financial support. Major decisions are often made collectively, with the welfare of the group taking precedence over individual interests.

Modesty and humility

In Malaysian culture, modesty and humility are highly regarded. Individuals are expected to be humble about their achievements and avoid overt displays of wealth or success, as this can be perceived as boastful or arrogant.

Social Norms

Malaysia's social norms are influenced by its religious and cultural values. Some of the most notable norms include:

Dress code

Due to the influence of Islam, modest dressing is encouraged in Malaysia, particularly for women. While the dress code is more relaxed in urban areas, it is essential to dress conservatively when visiting religious sites or attending formal events.

Greetings

In Malaysia, greetings often involve a handshake followed by placing the right hand over the heart. For Muslims, it is customary for men and women to avoid physical contact when greeting someone of the opposite gender.

Dining etiquette

Malaysians observe certain customs while dining, such as using the right hand for eating, as the left hand is considered unclean. It is also customary to wait for the host or the eldest person at the table to start eating before others begin.

Gift-giving

When visiting a Malaysian home, it is polite to bring a small gift, such as sweets or flowers. However, one should avoid giving gifts that are considered taboo in certain cultures, such as alcohol or pork products.

Language: Key Phrases and Expressions

Malaysia is a multilingual country with several languages spoken by its diverse population. The official language is Malay (also known as Bahasa Malaysia), while English is widely spoken as a second language. Additionally, other languages such as Mandarin, Tamil, and various indigenous languages are spoken by different ethnic communities. Here are some key phrases and expressions in Malay and English that can be useful when visiting Malaysia:

Malay (Bahasa Malaysia) Key Phrases:

- Selamat datang - Welcome
- Terima kasih - Thank you
- Sama-sama – You are welcome
- Maaf - Sorry
- Boleh saya bantu? - Can I help you?

- Ya - Yes
- Tidak - No
- Di mana tandas? - Where is the toilet?
- Berapa harganya? - How much does it cost?
- Saya tidak faham - I don't understand
- Tolong - Please help / Please
- Apa khabar? - How are you?
- Khabar baik - I'm fine
- Nama saya... - My name is...
- Jumpa lagi - See you again

Colloquial expressions

You might come across a mix of languages and colloquial expressions, often referred to as "Manglish" (a blend of Malay and English) or "Singlish" (a blend of Singaporean English and other languages). These expressions are commonly used in everyday conversations, especially among younger generations. Expats in Malaysia may find it helpful to familiarize themselves with some of these colloquial expressions to better understand informal conversations. Here are some common expressions you might hear:

- Lah: This is often added to the end of sentences or phrases for emphasis or to soften a statement. For example, "Come on, lah!" or "Don't worry, lah."
- Can or cannot: These words are often used to ask for or give permission, as in, "Can I borrow your pen?" or "Can, no problem."
- Tapau / bungkus: To take away food from a restaurant or stall. For example, "I want to tapau this nasi lemak."
- Makan: To eat. For example, "Let's go makan."
- Lepak: To hang out or spend time doing nothing in particular. For example, "We're just lepak-ing at the mall."
- Kiasu: A Hokkien term that translates to "afraid to lose" and is used to describe someone who is overly competitive or afraid of missing out. For example, "She's so kiasu, she always has to be the first in line."
- Boss: A friendly way to address someone, usually in a service setting. For example, "Boss, one teh tarik, please."
- Got / No got: Used to ask if something is available or not. For example, "Got tissue paper?" or "No got lah, finished already."

Famous Malaysian Myths and legends

- **Hang Tuah**: Legendary Malay warrior known for his loyalty and skill.
- **Puteri Gunung Ledang**: Enchanted princess residing atop Mount Ledang, seeking impossible dowry.
- Bidasari: Beautiful princess hidden in a fish, discovered by a king.
- **Mahsuri**: Wrongfully accused maiden, cursed Langkawi island upon her execution.
- **Hang Li Po**: Chinese princess married to Malacca's Sultan, symbol of diplomacy.
- **Batu Caves**: Revered Hindu site, home to powerful Lord Murugan statue.
- Puteri Santubong & Puteri Sejinjang: Mountain spirits turned into peaks after quarrelling.
- **Sang Kancil**: Clever mousedeer outsmarting predators, symbolizes wit and intelligence.

4. ADAPTING TO DAILY LIFE IN MALAYSIA

Housing and Accommodations

Moving to Malaysia can be an exciting experience, but it may also require some adjustment as you settle into your new home. One of the key aspects of adapting to daily life in Malaysia is finding suitable housing and accommodations. Here are some important factors to consider when looking for a place to live:

Types of accommodations

Malaysia offers a variety of housing options to suit different needs and budgets. These include apartments, condominiums, terrace houses, semi-detached houses, bungalows, and gated communities. Expats often prefer condominiums and serviced apartments due to the added amenities like swimming pools, gyms, and security services.

Location

When choosing a place to live, consider the location's proximity to your workplace, public transportation, schools, shopping centres, and healthcare facilities. Popular areas for expats in Kuala Lumpur, the capital city, include Mont Kiara, Bangsar, Damansara, and Ampang. In other cities like Penang and Johor Bahru, expats often choose residential areas close to international schools and business hubs.

Rental agreements

Rental agreements in Malaysia typically require a minimum one-year lease, with a security deposit equivalent to two months' rent and a utility deposit equivalent to half a month's rent. It's important to read the rental agreement carefully and clarify any terms or conditions you're unsure about. Be sure to negotiate any repairs or improvements with the landlord before signing the lease.

Cost of living

The cost of living in Malaysia is relatively low compared to Western countries, but housing costs can vary significantly depending on the location, type of accommodation, and amenities offered. In general, you can expect to pay more for accommodations in city centers and popular expat neighbourhoods. Be sure to factor in additional costs such as utilities, internet, and maintenance fees when budgeting for housing.

Finding accommodations

To find suitable housing, you can use online property websites, engage a real estate agent, or seek recommendations from fellow expats or colleagues. Real estate agents can be particularly helpful in navigating the local property market and negotiating rental terms on your behalf. Some popular property websites in Malaysia include iProperty, PropertyGuru, and Mudah.my.

Furnishings and utilities

Most rental properties in Malaysia come partially or fully furnished, but it's important to confirm what's included before signing the lease. In addition, you'll need to set up utilities such as electricity, water, and gas, as well as internet and cable TV services. The process for setting up utilities can vary depending on the provider, so it's a good idea to ask your landlord or real estate agent for assistance.

Transportation and Getting Around

Navigating the transportation system is an essential part of adapting to daily life in Malaysia. The country offers various modes of transportation, ranging from public transport to private vehicles. Here are some important aspects to consider when getting around in Malaysia:

Public transportation

Malaysia's public transportation system includes buses, trains, and taxis. In major cities like Kuala Lumpur, the Light Rail Transit (LRT), Mass Rapid Transit (MRT), and the KTM Komuter train service are reliable and efficient options for getting around. The monorail is another useful mode of transport in Kuala Lumpur, providing easy access to popular shopping and entertainment areas. Buses are widely available throughout the country, but they can sometimes be less reliable due to traffic congestion.

Taxis and ride-hailing apps

Taxis are a convenient way to get around in Malaysia, especially in urban areas. However, be aware that some taxi drivers may refuse to use the meter and instead charge a flat rate, which can be more expensive. To avoid this issue, you can use ride-hailing apps like Grab, which offer a more transparent pricing structure and the convenience of booking rides through your smartphone.

Driving

Many expats choose to drive in Malaysia, as it provides greater flexibility and convenience. Malaysia has an extensive road network, and driving is on the left side of the road. If you hold a valid driver's license from your home country or an international driving permit, you can drive in Malaysia for up to 90 days. After that, you'll need to obtain a Malaysian driver's license. Be prepared for heavy traffic, especially in urban areas, and be aware that driving habits may be different from what you're used to in your home country.

Motorbikes and scooters

Motorbikes and scooters are popular modes of transportation in Malaysia, especially for short distances and in congested areas. While they offer greater manoeuvrability and lower fuel costs, they can also be riskier due to the higher rate of accidents involving motorbikes. If you decide to use a motorbike or scooter, be sure to wear appropriate safety gear and follow local traffic rules.

Bicycle and e-scooter

Cycling and e-scooters are becoming more popular in Malaysia, particularly in urban areas with dedicated bicycle lanes and public bike-sharing programs. However, not all areas are cyclist-friendly, so it's essential to research local infrastructure and be cautious when sharing the road with motor vehicles.

Long-distance travel

For traveling long distances within Malaysia, you can choose between domestic flights, intercity buses, and trains. Domestic flights are the fastest and most convenient option for traveling between major cities and tourist destinations. Intercity buses are an affordable alternative, with numerous companies offering comfortable coaches and extensive routes. The train system in Malaysia, operated by KTM, provides a more leisurely way to travel, with options like the ETS (Electric Train Service) connecting major cities in Peninsular Malaysia.

Education and Schooling Options

Education is an important consideration for expats moving to Malaysia, especially those with children. Malaysia offers various schooling options, including public schools, private schools, international schools, and home-schooling. Here are some key factors to consider when choosing the right educational path for your family:

Public schools

Public schools in Malaysia follow the national curriculum, with Malay as the primary language of instruction. While public schools are accessible and affordable, they may not be the best option for expat children due to language barriers and differences in the curriculum compared to their home country.

Private schools

Private schools in Malaysia offer an alternative to public education, often with smaller class sizes and more personalized attention. Some private schools follow the Malaysian curriculum, while others may offer international curricula. The language of instruction in private schools is typically English, making them a more suitable option for expat children. However, private schools can be more expensive than public schools.

International schools

International schools are a popular choice for expat families in Malaysia. These schools cater specifically to the needs of expatriate students and follow international curricula such as the

International Baccalaureate (IB), Cambridge International Examinations (CIE), or the American, British, or Australian curricula. International schools generally have a diverse student body, high-quality facilities, and a strong focus on extracurricular activities. The main downside of international schools is the cost, as they can be significantly more expensive than public or private schools.

Home-schooling and online schooling

Home-schooling is another option for expat families in Malaysia. Home-schooling allows parents to have greater control over their child's education and tailor the curriculum to their specific needs. However, home-schooling requires a significant time commitment from parents and may limit children's opportunities for socialization with peers. It's essential to research local regulations and requirements for home-schooling before pursuing this option.

When choosing a school in Malaysia, consider factors such as:

- The curriculum offered and its compatibility with your child's educational background and future plans.
- The language of instruction and your child's language proficiency.
- School location, size, and facilities.
- Tuition fees and any additional costs, such as uniforms, books, and transportation.
- The school's reputation, accreditation, and performance in external examinations.

To find suitable schools, you can conduct online research, seek recommendations from fellow expats, or consult relocation experts. Once you have a shortlist of potential schools, it's a good idea to visit the schools in person and meet with administrators, teachers, and current students to get a feel for the school environment and make an informed decision.

By carefully considering your child's educational needs and researching the various schooling options available in Malaysia, you'll be better prepared to help them adapt to daily life in their new home.

Healthcare and Medical Facilities

Access to quality healthcare is a crucial aspect of adapting to daily life in Malaysia. The country boasts a well-developed healthcare system, with a mix of public and private medical facilities. Here are some key factors to consider when navigating the Malaysian healthcare system:

Public healthcare

Malaysia's public healthcare system is accessible and affordable, providing a wide range of services, including primary care, specialist care, and hospital care. Public hospitals and clinics are found in urban and rural areas throughout the country. Although the quality of care in public facilities is generally good, you may encounter longer waiting times, language barriers, and limited availability of certain treatments or procedures compared to private facilities.

Private healthcare

Private healthcare facilities in Malaysia offer high-quality care, state-of-the-art equipment, and a wider range of services than public facilities. Private hospitals and clinics are generally more expensive than public ones, but they often provide faster access to care and a higher level of patient comfort. Many private facilities cater to the expat community, with English-speaking staff and international accreditation. Major cities such as Kuala Lumpur, Penang, and Johor Bahru have numerous private hospitals and clinics.

Medical Specialists

If you require specialized care, both public and private hospitals in Malaysia have specialists in various fields such as cardiology, orthopaedics, and oncology. However, access to specialists may be more limited in rural areas. It's important to do thorough research and seek recommendations when selecting a specialist for your healthcare needs.

Pharmacies

Pharmacies are widely available in Malaysia, with many found in shopping centers, supermarkets, and stand-alone shops. Over-the-counter medications and personal care products are readily available, but prescription medications will require a doctor's prescription. It's a good idea to bring a sufficient supply of any essential prescription medications when moving to Malaysia and to familiarize yourself with the local equivalents or alternatives.

Health insurance

Expats living in Malaysia are advised to obtain comprehensive health insurance to cover the cost of private healthcare facilities, which can be expensive. Many employers provide health insurance as part of their benefits package, or you may choose to purchase an individual policy from a local or international insurance provider. Be sure to carefully review the coverage, limits, and exclusions of your insurance policy.

Emergency services

In case of a medical emergency, dial 999 for an ambulance. Emergency services in Malaysia are generally reliable, but response times may vary depending on your location. Be prepared to provide your name, address, and a description of the emergency when calling. It's essential to have a plan in place for emergencies, including knowing the location of the nearest hospital and having a list of emergency contacts.

Safety and Security

Safety and security are important factors when adapting to daily life in a new country. Overall, Malaysia is considered a safe destination for expats, with a relatively low crime rate. However, it's essential to be aware of potential risks and take appropriate precautions to ensure your personal safety and security. Here are some tips for staying safe in Malaysia:

Petty crime

As in any country, petty crime such as pickpocketing, purse-snatching, and theft can occur, particularly in crowded areas and tourist hotspots. To minimize the risk, be aware of your surroundings, keep your belongings secure, and avoid displaying valuable items like expensive jewellery or electronics. Be cautious when using ATMs, and opt for machines in well-lit, busy areas.

Road safety

Traffic accidents are a significant concern in Malaysia. Driving habits and road conditions may be different from what you're used to in your home country. If you choose to drive, familiarize yourself with local traffic rules, be cautious on the road, and always wear a seatbelt. For pedestrians, use designated crossings, and be vigilant when walking near traffic.

Personal safety

While Malaysia is generally safe for expats, it's essential to take basic precautions to protect yourself. Avoid walking alone in poorly lit or unfamiliar areas, especially at night. If you feel unsafe, trust your instincts and remove yourself from the situation. Be cautious when accepting offers of assistance from strangers and be wary of potential scams targeting tourists and expats.

Home security

To protect your home from break-ins, ensure that all doors and windows are secure and consider installing a home security system. Get to know your neighbours, as they can be valuable sources of information and support in case of emergencies.

Natural disasters

Malaysia is prone to certain natural disasters, such as flooding during the monsoon season and occasional landslides in hilly areas. Familiarize yourself with the risks in your area and be prepared to follow local authorities' advice in case of an emergency. Develop an emergency plan and have a basic disaster supplies kit on hand.

Health and safety

Maintain good personal hygiene and follow local guidelines to prevent the spread of illnesses such as dengue fever and COVID-19. Be aware of the risk of heatstroke and dehydration in

Malaysia's tropical climate, and take precautions such as staying hydrated and wearing sunscreen.

Emergency services

In case of emergency, dial 999 for police, ambulance, or fire services. Keep a list of emergency contacts, including your home country's embassy or consulate, your healthcare provider, and any personal emergency contacts.

possible.

Register with your embassy

Register with your home country's embassy to receive updates on safety and security information.

5. NAVIGATING SOCIAL INTERACTIONS AI ETIQUETTE

Making Friends and Building Connections

Navigating social interactions and etiquette is an important aspect of adapting to daily life in another country. Building connections and making friends with locals and other expatriates can greatly enhance your experience and help you acclimate to the culture more quickly. Here are some tips for making friends and building connections while respecting local social etiquette:

Language

Learning some basic phrases can go a long way in making friends and breaking down communication barriers. Even if your language skills are limited, locals will appreciate your effort to speak their language. Additionally, consider enrolling in a language class, which can also serve as an opportunity to meet new people and practice your language skills.

Cultural understanding

Familiarize yourself with local customs, traditions, and social norms to better understand and navigate social interactions. Being aware of and respecting local etiquette, such as greetings, table manners, and gift-giving customs, will help you make a positive impression and build rapport with locals.

Networking events and social clubs

Attend networking events, expatriate meetups, and social clubs to meet like-minded individuals and expand your social circle. There are numerous groups and organizations catering to expatriates, offering opportunities for cultural exchange, language practice, and shared interests.

Hobbies and interests

Pursue your hobbies and interests by joining clubs, teams, or classes. Participating in activities that you enjoy will provide a natural setting to connect with others who share your interests, making it easier to build friendships.

Social media and messaging apps

Social media platforms and messaging apps are usually widely used and can be an excellent tool for staying connected and organizing social events. Be sure to exchange contact information with new acquaintances and join relevant groups to stay informed about upcoming events and activities.

Be open and approachable

When interacting with locals and other expatriates, be open, approachable, and willing to engage in conversation. Share your experiences, ask questions, and show genuine interest in learning about culture and the experiences of others. Demonstrating curiosity and an open-minded attitude will make you more approachable and help you build connections more easily.

Patience and persistence

Building meaningful friendships takes time and effort, especially when navigating cultural differences. Be patient and persistent in your efforts to connect with others and remember that building strong relationships may require additional time and understanding.

Social Customs and Taboos

Malaysia is a multicultural and diverse country, with Malay, Chinese, Indian, and various indigenous ethnic groups coexisting harmoniously. Understanding and respecting the social customs and taboos of each group is crucial for successful interactions and avoiding unintentional offense. Here are some key social customs and taboos to be aware of while in Malaysia:

Greetings

In Malaysia, the traditional Malay greeting is the "salam" – a gentle touch of the hands, followed by placing your right hand over your heart. However, many Malaysians use a simple handshake as a standard greeting. Be aware that some conservative Muslims may avoid physical contact with members of the opposite sex. Always greet the eldest person first as a sign of respect.

Dress conservatively

Malaysia is predominantly a Muslim country, and dressing modestly is essential, particularly for women. Avoid wearing revealing clothing, especially when visiting religious sites, and dress professionally in business settings.

Remove your shoes

When entering a Malaysian home or a place of worship, it is customary to remove your shoes. This is a sign of respect and also helps to keep the indoors clean.

Respect religious practices

Malaysia is a multicultural society with various religious beliefs. Be respectful of different religious customs, particularly during prayer times and religious festivals. Avoid eating in public during the daytime in the Muslim fasting month of Ramadan.

Giving and receiving

When giving or receiving items, particularly gifts or business cards, use your right hand or both hands. The left hand is considered unclean in Muslim culture and should not be used to pass objects to others.

Table manners

When dining, wait to be seated by the host and follow their lead during the meal. Malaysians traditionally eat with their hands, particularly in Malay homes. If you choose to do the same, use your right hand only. It is polite to try a little bit of each dish, but avoid taking the last portion from a shared plate.

Public displays of affection

Malaysia is a conservative country, and public displays of affection are generally frowned upon, especially among the Muslim population. Keep physical contact to a minimum in public spaces to avoid causing discomfort to others.

Avoid discussing sensitive topics

To maintain harmony, Malaysians tend to avoid discussing sensitive subjects such as race, religion, or politics. Be cautious when engaging in conversations about these topics and respect differing viewpoints.

Do not point with your index finger

Pointing with your index finger is considered rude in Malaysia. Instead, use your thumb with your other fingers folded or gesture with an open palm.

Respect the national flag and symbols

Malaysians are proud of their national symbols, and it's essential to show respect for the flag, national anthem, and other symbols of the country.

Gift-Giving Etiquette

In Malaysia, gift-giving is an important aspect of social and business relationships. It helps to foster goodwill, respect, and appreciation. The following are some general guidelines for gift-giving etiquette in Malaysia:

Occasions

Gifts are typically given on occasions such as religious festivals, weddings, housewarmings, and birthdays. In a business setting, gifts may be exchanged after the successful completion of a project, during the festive seasons, or as a token of appreciation.

Selecting a gift

Choose modest yet thoughtful gifts that reflect your respect and appreciation for the recipient. Common gifts include chocolates, pastries, or handicraft items. For business associates, consider office accessories, small electronic gadgets, or local souvenirs.

Cultural considerations

Be mindful of the recipient's cultural and religious background when selecting a gift. Avoid giving alcohol to Muslim recipients, as it is forbidden in Islam. Similarly, avoid giving non-halal food items or products made from animal skins to Muslims.

Presentation

Wrap the gift neatly and in colourful or festive wrapping paper. In Malaysia, colours like green, blue, or yellow are well-received, while white and black should be avoided as they are associated with mourning and funerals.

Handing over the gift

When giving or receiving a gift, it is customary to use both hands or your right hand. This gesture shows respect and is especially important when interacting with elders or people of higher status.

Timing

In a social setting, it is best to present the gift upon arrival or when leaving. In a business setting, gifts are usually exchanged at the end of a meeting or after a successful project completion.

Reciprocation

Malaysians may reciprocate with a gift of equal or lesser value to show their appreciation. It is not necessary to reciprocate immediately; doing so at a later time is acceptable.

Opening gifts

It is customary to wait and open the gift later in private rather than in front of the giver. This gesture shows modesty and prevents any potential embarrassment if the gift is not well-received.

Dining and Food Culture

Malaysia's dining and food culture is a reflection of its diverse population, which includes Malays, Chinese, Indians, and indigenous groups. This cultural mix has resulted in a rich culinary landscape, with each group contributing their unique flavours, ingredients, and cooking techniques. Here are some key aspects of Malaysian dining and food culture:

Variety of cuisines

Malaysia is known for its wide variety of dishes, ranging from Malay, Chinese, and Indian to Nyonya (a blend of Malay and Chinese), and indigenous cuisines. Popular dishes include nasi lemak, roti canai, char kway teow, and laksa.

Shared dining

Meals are typically communal, with various dishes shared among family members or friends. It is common for everyone to serve themselves from the shared plates, either using their hands or utensils.

Eating with hands

Traditional Malay and Indian meals are often eaten with hands, specifically the right hand. This is considered a more intimate and enjoyable way to experience the food. However, utensils are also widely used, especially in urban areas and when consuming Chinese or Western dishes.

Rice as a staple

Rice is the main staple in Malaysia, with most meals including some form of rice, whether it is steamed, fried, or in the form of noodles.

Halal food

Due to the significant Muslim population, many Malaysian dishes are halal, meaning they comply with Islamic dietary laws. Pork is generally avoided in Malay cuisine, while Chinese and Indian cuisine might offer halal and non-halal options.

Street food

Malaysia is famous for its street food culture, particularly at night markets or hawker centers. These bustling food hubs offer a wide variety of dishes at affordable prices.

Tea and coffee culture

Malaysians enjoy their tea (teh tarik) and coffee (kopi), which are commonly consumed at local coffee shops known as "kopitiams." These establishments serve as social hubs, where people gather to chat, eat, and relax.

Spicy food

Many Malaysian dishes are spicy, using ingredients such as chili peppers, curry, and **sambal** (a chili-based condiment). However, there are also milder options for those with a lower tolerance for heat.

Dining etiquette

When dining with Malaysians, it is important to respect cultural norms, such as waiting for the host to begin eating before starting your meal, not pointing with your utensils, and avoiding discussions of sensitive topics during the meal.

Festive food

During festivals and celebrations, Malaysian households prepare special dishes that hold cultural significance. For example, during **Hari Raya Aidilfitri**, **ketupat** (rice cakes cooked in woven palm leaves) and **rendang** (a slow-cooked, spiced meat dish) are often served.

6. BUSINESS ETIQUETTE AND PRACTICES

Building Trust and Relationships

In Malaysia, building trust and maintaining relationships are essential aspects of conducting successful business. The Malaysian business culture values personal connections and face-to-face interactions, which play a significant role in establishing credibility and fostering collaboration. Here are some tips for building trust and relationships in Malaysian business settings:

Initial introductions

Leverage personal connections or introductions through mutual contacts, as these can help establish trust and credibility from the outset. Malaysians place importance on knowing someone directly or through a known intermediary.

Respect hierarchy

The Malaysian business culture is hierarchical, with decisions often made by senior management. Show respect to individuals of higher status by addressing them with their honorific titles (e.g., Dato, Datin, Tan Sri) and their full name or surname.

Face-to-face meetings

Personal interactions are highly valued in Malaysia, so make an effort to arrange face-to-face meetings whenever possible. These meetings help build rapport, establish trust, and demonstrate commitment to the business relationship.

Business cards

Exchange business cards with both hands or your right hand, and take a moment to read the card before putting it away respectfully. This gesture demonstrates respect and interest in the person you are meeting.

Small talk

Engage in small talk and personal conversations before diving into business matters. This helps to build rapport and strengthen relationships. Topics may include family, travel experiences, or food.

Patience and indirect communication

Malaysians may communicate in a more indirect and polite manner to avoid potential confrontation or loss of face. Be patient, diplomatic, and mindful of non-verbal cues to ensure effective communication.

Group harmony

The Malaysian business culture prioritizes group harmony and consensus. Avoid confrontation or aggressive negotiation tactics, as these can damage relationships and jeopardize future collaboration.

Socializing

Accept invitations to social events, as these provide opportunities to network and build personal connections outside the office environment. Be prepared to discuss non-business topics and to share information about your own background.

Gift-giving

Giving small gifts as a token of appreciation or to mark a successful business deal is common in Malaysia. Ensure the gifts are culturally appropriate, modest, and not too extravagant to avoid causing embarrassment.

Follow-up and nurture relationships

After your initial meetings, maintain regular contact and follow up on any commitments made. Building and nurturing relationships is a long-term process in Malaysia, and continued communication is key to fostering trust and collaboration.

Dress Code and Appearance

In Malaysia, dressing appropriately and maintaining a professional appearance are important aspects of conducting business. A well-groomed and modest appearance is valued, as it reflects respect for oneself, others, and the business environment. Here are some guidelines on dress code and appearance in Malaysian business settings:

Formal attire

Business attire in Malaysia is generally conservative and formal. For men, a suit with a tie is the standard dress code, while for women, a knee-length skirt or dress, or a pantsuit with a blouse, is considered appropriate.

Colours

Stick to neutral or dark colours for suits and dresses, such as black, grey, or navy blue. Bright colours should generally be reserved for more casual settings or festive occasions.

Modesty

Women should dress modestly, covering their shoulders and avoiding revealing necklines or overly tight clothing. Skirts should be at least knee-length. This is particularly important when interacting with conservative Muslim clients or colleagues.

Lightweight fabrics

Due to the hot and humid climate in Malaysia, choose lightweight fabrics such as cotton, linen, or light wool to stay comfortable while maintaining a professional appearance.

Footwear

Closed-toe shoes are recommended for both men and women in business settings. Men should wear dress shoes, while women can wear conservative pumps or flats.

Accessories

Keep accessories to a minimum and avoid flashy or ostentatious jewellery. A simple wristwatch, belt, or small earrings are acceptable. Ensure that any accessories are in good condition and coordinate well with your outfit.

Personal grooming

Maintain a well-groomed appearance, with neatly styled hair and conservative makeup for women. Men should be clean-shaven or have well-trimmed facial hair. Strong fragrances should be avoided.

Religious considerations

Be mindful of the cultural and religious backgrounds of your Malaysian counterparts. For example, when interacting with Muslim colleagues, it is essential to dress modestly and respect their customs, such as not shaking hands with the opposite gender unless initiated by them.

Business Cards and Introductions

Exchanging business cards and making introductions are important aspects of Malaysian business culture. These interactions serve as an opportunity to establish credibility, demonstrate respect, and set the tone for future business dealings. Here are some guidelines for exchanging business cards and making introductions in Malaysia:

Business cards

Have plenty of business cards on hand, preferably with one side in English and the other side in Bahasa Malaysia, the national language. This demonstrates respect for the local culture and ensures clarity in communication.

Presenting business cards

When presenting your business card, use both hands or your right hand, with the text facing the recipient. This gesture shows respect and is an essential part of Malaysian business etiquette.

Receiving business cards

When receiving a business card, accept it with both hands or your right hand. Take a moment to read the card and acknowledge the person's name and title before carefully placing the card in a cardholder or on the table, if you are seated. Avoid hastily putting the card away, as this can be perceived as disrespectful.

Introductions

In a business setting, introductions usually follow a hierarchical order, starting with the most senior person present. Wait for your Malaysian counterpart to initiate the introduction, and follow their lead.

Addressing others

Address people by their honorific titles (e.g., Dato, Datin, Tan Sri) followed by their full name or surname. If they do not have an honorific title, use the appropriate courtesy title, such as Mr., Mrs., or Miss, followed by their surname. Avoid using first names unless specifically invited to do so.

Handshakes

A handshake is the standard form of greeting in Malaysian business settings. However, be mindful of religious customs, especially when interacting with Muslim colleagues. Some conservative Muslims may prefer not to shake hands with the opposite gender. In such cases, it is appropriate to place your right hand over your heart and give a slight bow or nod as a gesture of respect.

Business introductions

When introducing yourself, state your full name, title, and the organization you represent. Speak clearly and maintain eye contact to show confidence and sincerity.

Small talk

Engaging in small talk before delving into business discussions is common in Malaysia. This helps to build rapport and establish trust. Appropriate topics for small talk include family, travel, food, and sports.

Communication Styles and Nonverbal Cues

In Malaysia, understanding communication styles and being aware of nonverbal cues are essential to successful business interactions. Malaysian communication can be characterized as polite, indirect, and relationship-oriented. Here are some key aspects of communication styles and nonverbal cues in Malaysia:

Indirect communication

Malaysians often communicate in a more indirect and subtle manner to maintain group harmony and avoid confrontation. This means they may avoid expressing disagreement or negative opinions outright, instead conveying their message through nonverbal cues or gentle suggestions.

High-context culture

Malaysia is a high-context culture, where much of the communication is conveyed through nonverbal cues, shared understanding, and implied meaning. It's essential to pay attention to tone, body language, and facial expressions to fully comprehend the message being conveyed.

Nonverbal cues

Common nonverbal cues in Malaysia include a smile to express agreement, pleasure, or discomfort; a slight nod to indicate understanding or acknowledgment; and avoiding direct eye contact to show respect, especially when interacting with elders or superiors.

Silence

Silence is considered an essential aspect of communication in Malaysia. It allows for reflection and thought before responding, and it may also signal disagreement or discomfort. Be patient and wait for your Malaysian counterparts to respond, avoiding the temptation to fill the silence.

Polite language

Malaysians often use polite language and address people with respect, using honorific titles and formal expressions. This formality may decrease as relationships develop, but it is important to maintain a respectful tone in initial interactions.

Avoiding confrontation

In Malaysian business culture, maintaining face and group harmony is highly valued. Consequently, confrontation or direct criticism should be avoided. If you need to address an issue, do so diplomatically, using suggestions or indirect language to preserve the relationship.

Gestures

Use gestures cautiously, as some may have different meanings in Malaysia. For example, pointing with the index finger is considered impolite; instead, use your thumb or an open palm to gesture towards something. Avoid crossing your arms or placing your hands on your hips, as these gestures may be perceived as aggressive or disrespectful.

Personal space

Be mindful of personal space when interacting with Malaysian colleagues. Maintain an appropriate distance during conversations, and avoid touching others unless you have a close relationship or are following local customs, such as handshakes or placing your hand on someone's shoulder during a group photo.

7. OFFICE CULTURE AND HIERARCHIES

Respect for Authority and Seniority

In Malaysia, office culture is shaped by the values of respect for authority, seniority, and hierarchy. These values are deeply ingrained in Malaysian society and have a significant influence on workplace interactions and decision-making processes. Here are some key aspects of office culture and hierarchies in Malaysia:

Respect for authority

Malaysians generally have a strong respect for authority figures, such as managers, supervisors, and company leaders. Employees are expected to show deference to those in positions of power and follow their guidance without question.

Seniority

Seniority plays a crucial role in the Malaysian workplace, with older or more experienced employees often holding higher positions and greater authority. Employees are expected to show respect for their seniors, both in terms of age and experience, by addressing them with appropriate titles and listening to their opinions.

Hierarchy

The Malaysian office culture is hierarchical, with decision-making authority concentrated at the top levels of management. Lower-ranking employees are generally expected to carry out their tasks without challenging the decisions made by their superiors. This hierarchy also extends to workplace interactions, with senior staff members often leading conversations and being served first during meals or refreshment breaks.

Consensus building

Despite the emphasis on hierarchy, Malaysian organizations often strive to reach a consensus in decision-making processes. This can involve lengthy discussions and meetings, as everyone's opinion is considered and the group works together to find a solution that maintains harmony and balance.

Face-saving

Preserving one's reputation or "face" is crucial in Malaysian office culture. Public criticism or confrontation is generally avoided to prevent embarrassment or loss of face. Instead, issues are addressed privately and diplomatically to maintain positive working relationships.

Group orientation

Malaysians have a strong sense of group identity and loyalty, valuing collaboration and teamwork over individual achievements. Employees are expected to contribute to the success of the group and support their colleagues in achieving common goals.

Relationship building

Establishing personal connections and building trust are vital aspects of Malaysian office culture. Employees often engage in small talk and share personal stories to foster rapport and strengthen working relationships. Participating in social events and informal gatherings outside the office is also encouraged to deepen these connections.

8. BUSINESS MEETINGS AND NEGOTIATIONS

Scheduling and Punctuality

Business meetings and negotiations in Malaysia involve certain cultural nuances that can impact their success. Scheduling and punctuality are important aspects to consider in order to establish a positive working relationship with your Malaysian counterparts. Here are some guidelines regarding scheduling and punctuality for business meetings and negotiations in Malaysia:

Scheduling meetings

Schedule meetings at least two weeks in advance, providing a clear agenda to allow your Malaysian colleagues enough time to prepare. Avoid scheduling meetings during major religious or national holidays, as well as during prayer times for Muslim counterparts.

Confirming meetings

Due to the possibility of unforeseen schedule changes, it is a good practice to confirm the meeting date, time, and location a few days before the scheduled appointment.

Punctuality

While punctuality is generally appreciated in Malaysia, it's essential to be aware that traffic congestion, particularly in urban areas, can sometimes cause delays. It's important to be understanding if your Malaysian colleagues arrive late. However, as a foreign guest, it's crucial for you to arrive on time or slightly early to demonstrate respect and commitment.

Starting meetings

Meetings often begin with some small talk to build rapport and establish a comfortable atmosphere before delving into business matters. Be prepared to engage in conversation about family, travel, or local culture to strengthen your relationships with your Malaysian colleagues.

Meeting dynamics

Malaysian business meetings can be formal and structured, with an emphasis on respect for hierarchy. Wait for the most senior person to initiate discussions, and allow them to lead the conversation. Be prepared for a more indirect communication style and avoid confrontation during negotiations.

Decision-making

In Malaysian business culture, decision-making tends to be hierarchical, with the final decision resting with the top-level management. Keep in mind that the process may be slower than you are used to, as reaching consensus among all relevant parties is highly valued.

Follow-up

After the meeting, it is essential to send a follow-up email summarizing the key points discussed and outlining the next steps. This not only demonstrates your commitment to the business relationship but also ensures that everyone is on the same page.

Meeting Structure and Protocol

Understanding the meeting structure and protocol in Malaysia is important for successful business interactions. Being mindful of the cultural norms will enable you to navigate meetings effectively and develop strong relationships with your Malaysian counterparts. Here are some guidelines regarding meeting structure and protocol in Malaysia:

Introductions

Introductions are typically made in order of seniority, starting with the highest-ranking person present. Wait for your Malaysian counterpart to initiate the introduction and follow their lead. Address people using their honorific titles, if applicable, or use Mr., Mrs., or Miss followed by their surname.

Business cards

Exchange business cards at the beginning of the meeting, preferably with one side printed in English and the other side in Bahasa Malaysia. Present your card with both hands or your right hand, and take a moment to read the card you receive before placing it in a cardholder or on the table.

Seating arrangements

Seating in Malaysian business meetings often follows a hierarchical order, with the highest-ranking individuals seated at the head of the table. Wait to be shown your seat, or ask your host where they would like you to sit.

Agenda

Meetings in Malaysia typically follow a structured agenda, with discussions led by the most senior person present. Ensure that you provide a clear agenda in advance, allowing your Malaysian colleagues enough time to prepare.

Small talk

Engaging in small talk before starting the formal meeting agenda is common in Malaysia. This helps to build rapport and establish trust. Topics for small talk may include family, travel, food, and sports.

Presentation materials

When giving a presentation, provide clear and concise visual aids, such as slides or handouts, to support your points. This will help your Malaysian counterparts follow your presentation more easily and facilitate better understanding.

Indirect communication

Malaysians often communicate in an indirect manner, valuing group harmony and avoiding confrontation. Pay attention to nonverbal cues and implied meaning, and be prepared to read between the lines to understand the message being conveyed.

Decision-making

Decision-making in Malaysia tends to be hierarchical and can be slower compared to some Western countries. Patience and persistence are crucial in negotiations, as reaching a consensus among all parties is highly valued.

Closing the meeting

At the end of the meeting, thank your hosts and participants for their time and contributions. It is essential to follow up with a summary of the meeting, outlining the agreed-upon actions and next steps.

Tips for Effective Negotiation

Effective negotiation in Malaysia requires an understanding of cultural norms and expectations. Here are some tips to help you negotiate successfully with your Malaysian counterparts:

Relationship building

Establishing personal connections and trust is crucial in Malaysia. Invest time in getting to know your counterparts through small talk, social events, or informal gatherings before entering into negotiations.

Patience

Decision-making in Malaysia can be slower than in some Western countries, as reaching a consensus among all parties is highly valued. Be patient, avoid pushing for immediate decisions, and be prepared for multiple rounds of negotiation.

Indirect communication

Malaysians often communicate in an indirect manner to maintain group harmony and avoid confrontation. Pay attention to nonverbal cues, tone of voice, and implied meaning, and be prepared to read between the lines.

Face-saving

Preserving one's reputation or "face" is essential in Malaysian culture. Avoid public criticism, confrontation, or putting your counterparts on the spot. Address issues privately and diplomatically to maintain positive working relationships.

Respect for hierarchy

Show respect for the hierarchy within the Malaysian organization by addressing senior members with appropriate titles and giving them the opportunity to lead the conversation. Be prepared to negotiate with several levels of management, as the final decision often rests with the top-level management.

Flexibility

Be open to adapting your negotiation strategy and approach as needed. Listen to the concerns and suggestions of your Malaysian counterparts and be willing to compromise to reach a mutually beneficial agreement.

Clear communication

Provide clear and concise information, supported by visual aids or written documents, to help your counterparts understand your proposals and expectations. Avoid using jargon or complex terminology that may cause confusion.

Reciprocity

Malaysian negotiators often value reciprocity and may expect concessions in return for those they offer. Be prepared to give and take during the negotiation process to foster a sense of balance and fairness.

Closing the deal

Once an agreement is reached, it is essential to follow up with a written contract outlining the terms and conditions. This will help to avoid misunderstandings and ensure that both parties are on the same page.

Post-negotiation relationship

Maintain contact with your Malaysian counterparts after the negotiation is complete, as ongoing communication and relationship building are key to long-term business success in Malaysia.

Common Mistakes to Avoid

When conducting business in Malaysia, it's important to be aware of potential pitfalls and cultural faux pas. Here are some common mistakes to avoid when engaging in business activities in Malaysia:

Ignoring hierarchy

Failing to acknowledge the importance of hierarchy and seniority in the Malaysian workplace can lead to misunderstandings and strained relationships. Always show respect to those in higher positions and address them with appropriate titles.

Overlooking relationship building

Underestimating the value of personal connections and trust can hinder your business success. Take the time to get to know your Malaysian counterparts and invest in building strong working relationships.

Being too direct

Using overly direct communication or confrontational language can be off-putting to your Malaysian colleagues, as they typically favour a more indirect and subtle communication style. Adapt your approach to maintain harmony and avoid causing offense.

Neglecting nonverbal cues

Failing to pay attention to body language, facial expressions, and tone of voice can lead to miscommunication. Be aware of these nonverbal cues and consider their impact on your interactions.

Inappropriate gestures

Unintentionally using gestures that are considered rude or offensive in Malaysia, such as pointing with your index finger or placing your hands on your hips, can create a negative impression. Be mindful of your gestures and follow local customs.

Disregarding religious sensitivities

Overlooking the importance of religion in Malaysia can lead to cultural misunderstandings. Be respectful of religious practices, such as prayer times and dietary restrictions, and avoid scheduling meetings during religious holidays.

Impatience

Expecting quick decision-making can be counterproductive in Malaysia, where reaching a consensus among all parties is highly valued. Be patient and persistent in your negotiations, and be prepared for a slower decision-making process.

Inadequate follow-up

Failing to follow up on agreements and discussions can lead to confusion and missed opportunities. Ensure that you send a summary of meetings and outline the next steps to maintain momentum and demonstrate your commitment to the business relationship.

Inappropriate attire

Dressing too casually or inappropriately can create a negative impression in Malaysian business settings. Follow local dress codes, opting for conservative and professional attire.

Underestimating the importance of face-saving

Public criticism or confrontation can cause your Malaysian counterparts to lose face, which can have a detrimental effect on your working relationship. Address issues privately and diplomatically to preserve harmony and maintain positive relationships.

9. BUSINESS DINING AND ENTERTAINMENT

Traditional Hospitality

Traditional Malaysian hospitality is rooted in the country's diverse cultural heritage, which includes influences from Malay, Chinese, Indian, and indigenous communities. Warmth, generosity, and a strong emphasis on making guests feel welcome and comfortable are key aspects of Malaysian hospitality. Here are some characteristics of traditional hospitality in Malaysia:

Warm welcome

Malaysians are known for their friendly and warm demeanour, often greeting guests with a smile and a handshake. The traditional Malay greeting, "Salam," involves a light touch of the hands followed by placing your right hand on your heart, symbolizing sincerity and respect.

Respectful gestures

Traditional Malaysian hospitality emphasizes showing respect to guests, such as addressing them with appropriate honorifics or titles, offering a seat of honour, and ensuring that the guest's needs are attended to promptly.

Food and refreshments

Malaysians are passionate about food, and it plays a central role in traditional hospitality. Guests are often treated to an array of local dishes, snacks, and refreshments, and hosts will ensure that their guests are well-fed and satisfied. It is customary to accept food and drink offered to you as a sign of politeness and appreciation.

Sharing culture and traditions

Malaysian hosts take pride in sharing their culture and traditions with guests, often through storytelling, music, dance, or showcasing local handicrafts. Participating in these activities and showing interest in learning about Malaysian culture will strengthen the bond between you and your hosts.

Home visits

If you are invited to a Malaysian home, it is customary to bring a small gift, such as chocolates, sweets, or flowers, as a token of appreciation for the host's hospitality. Upon entering the home, it is polite to remove your shoes. Be mindful of religious and cultural sensitivities, such as dietary restrictions and prayer times, during your visit.

Reciprocity

Malaysian hospitality often involves a sense of reciprocity, and guests are expected to return the kindness and warmth extended by their hosts. This can be achieved through expressing gratitude, offering compliments, or reciprocating with an invitation or a small gift.

Emphasis on group harmony

A key aspect of Malaysian hospitality is the emphasis on group harmony and maintaining positive relationships. Avoid discussing sensitive topics or engaging in confrontational behaviour that might disrupt the harmony of the gathering.

10. LEISURE, ENTERTAINMENT AND FAMILY ACTIVITIES

Exploring Natural Wonders

Malaysia is blessed with a wealth of natural wonders that showcase the country's diverse landscapes and rich biodiversity. From pristine beaches and lush rainforests to towering mountains and mysterious caves, there are numerous natural attractions worth exploring in Malaysia:

Mount Kinabalu

Located in Sabah, Borneo, **Mount Kinabalu** is the highest peak in Malaysia and a UNESCO World Heritage Site. The mountain is famous for its unique flora and fauna, and attracts hikers and climbers from around the world.

Taman Negara

This national park is one of the world's oldest rainforests, estimated to be over 130 million years old. Home to an incredible array of plant and animal species, **Taman Negara** offers numerous activities such as jungle trekking, canopy walks, and wildlife watching.

Cameron Highlands

Known for its cool climate, tea plantations, and verdant landscapes, the **Cameron Highlands** is a popular destination for nature lovers. Visitors can explore the area's many hiking trails, visit strawberry farms, and enjoy the stunning views of the rolling hills.

Langkawi

An archipelago of 99 islands, **Langkawi** boasts pristine beaches, crystal-clear waters, and lush rainforests. The UNESCO-listed Langkawi Geopark is home to unique geological formations, mangroves, and diverse wildlife, making it a paradise for nature enthusiasts.

Bako National Park

Located in Sarawak, Borneo, **Bako National Park** is the oldest national park in Malaysia. It features diverse ecosystems, including rainforests, mangroves, and coastal areas, providing a habitat for various plant and animal species, such as the rare proboscis monkey.

Sipadan Island

Renowned for its world-class scuba diving, **Sipadan Island** is a haven for marine life, including turtles, sharks, and colourful coral reefs. The island is a protected area with limited permits available for divers, ensuring the preservation of its natural beauty.

Gunung Mulu National Park

A UNESCO World Heritage Site in Sarawak, Borneo, **Gunung Mulu National Park** is famous for its dramatic limestone karst formations and extensive cave systems. Highlights include the Deer Cave, Clearwater Cave, and the striking Pinnacles rock formation.

Perhentian Islands

These **idyllic islands** offer crystal-clear waters, powdery white sand beaches, and vibrant coral reefs, making them a popular destination for snorkelling, scuba diving, and relaxation.

Royal Belum State Park

Located in Perak, this **ancient rainforest reserve** is home to rare wildlife, such as Malayan tigers, Asian elephants, and the Rafflesia, the world's largest flower. The park offers activities like wildlife watching, trekking, and birdwatching.

Danum Valley

A pristine rainforest reserve in Sabah, Borneo, **Danum Valley** is a haven for wildlife enthusiasts, offering the opportunity to spot orangutans, gibbons, and various bird species. Visitors can explore the area through jungle trekking, canopy walks, and night safaris.

Historic Sites and Cultural Attractions

Malaysia is a country steeped in history and cultural diversity, offering numerous historic sites and cultural attractions that provide a glimpse into its rich heritage. Here are some of the most notable sites and attractions to explore in Malaysia:

Malacca

A UNESCO World Heritage Site, Malacca is a historic city that has been influenced by Malay, Chinese, Indian, Portuguese, Dutch, and British cultures. Key attractions include St. Paul's Hill, A Famosa Fort, and Jonker Street.

Penang

Known as the "Pearl of the Orient," Penang is another UNESCO World Heritage Site with a rich cultural heritage. Explore George Town's colonial architecture, visit Kek Lok Si Temple, and stroll along Armenian Street.

Batu Caves

A series of limestone caves and Hindu temples located just outside Kuala Lumpur, Batu Caves is a popular destination for both tourists and pilgrims. The site features a giant golden statue of Lord Murugan and colourful staircases leading to the caves.

Kellie's Castle

Situated in Perak, **Kellie's Castle** is a unique Scottish-inspired mansion built by a Scottish planter in the early 20th century. Visitors can explore the unfinished castle, which has become a popular spot for photography and history enthusiasts.

Islamic Arts Museum Malaysia

Located in Kuala Lumpur, this museum showcases a vast collection of Islamic art and artifacts, including textiles, ceramics, and manuscripts. It offers a fascinating insight into the history and culture of Islamic civilizations.

Sarawak Cultural Village

This living museum in Sarawak, Borneo, provides a glimpse into the traditional lifestyles of various ethnic groups in Malaysia, including the Iban, Bidayuh, and Orang Ulu. Visitors can watch cultural performances, participate in traditional crafts, and sample local cuisine.

Sultan Abdul Samad Building

A historic building in Kuala Lumpur, the **Sultan Abdul Samad Building** features stunning Moorish-style architecture and serves as a backdrop for important events such as Malaysia's National Day Parade.

Ipoh Old Town

Ipoh is a charming city known for its well-preserved colonial architecture and historic sites, such as the Railway Station, Birch Memorial Clock Tower, and Concubine Lane.

A' Famosa

Located in Malacca, A' Famosa is a 16th-century Portuguese fort and one of the oldest European architectural remains in Southeast Asia. The surviving gatehouse, Porta de Santiago, is a popular attraction for history buffs.

Perak Royal Museum

Housed in a former palace, the Perak Royal Museum showcases the history and culture of the state of Perak, featuring royal regalia, artifacts, and a replica of the Perak throne.

Family-Friendly Activities and Entertainment

Malaysia offers a wide range of family-friendly activities and entertainment options that cater to various interests and age groups. Here are some popular destinations and activities that you can enjoy with your family:

Sunway Lagoon

Located in Selangor, this multi-themed amusement park features water attractions, thrill rides, a wildlife park, and a Nickelodeon-themed area for younger children.

LEGOLAND Malaysia

Situated in Johor Bahru, LEGOLAND Malaysia is the first LEGO-themed park in Asia. It offers over 70 interactive rides, shows, and attractions, as well as a water park and SEA LIFE aquarium.

Aquaria KLCC

Located in Kuala Lumpur, Aquaria KLCC is an oceanarium that showcases over 5,000 aquatic and land-bound creatures. Highlights include a walk-through tunnel, touch pools, and various marine habitats.

KidZania Kuala Lumpur

This interactive, educational theme park in Kuala Lumpur allows children to role-play various careers, such as firefighter, pilot, or doctor, in a realistic, kid-sized city.

Kuala Lumpur Bird Park

Home to over 3,000 birds, this park is one of the world's largest covered bird parks. Visitors can explore walk-in aviaries, watch bird shows, and participate in feeding sessions.

Penang Hill

Ride the funicular railway to the top of Penang Hill, where you can enjoy panoramic views of George Town, explore lush gardens, and visit attractions like The Habitat nature park.

Farm in the City

This petting zoo in Seri Kembangan, Selangor, allows visitors to interact with various animals, such as rabbits, deer, and birds, in a village-style setting.

Langkawi SkyCab and SkyBridge

Enjoy a cable car ride to the top of Mount Mat Cincang in Langkawi and take a walk on the SkyBridge, a curved pedestrian bridge offering stunning views of the surrounding islands and rainforests.

Orangutan sanctuaries

Visit the Sepilok Orangutan Rehabilitation Centre in Sabah or the Semenggoh Wildlife Centre in Sarawak to learn about orangutan conservation efforts and watch these fascinating primates up close.

Lost World of Tambun

Located in Ipoh, this adventure park features water rides, amusement park attractions, a petting zoo, and a hot springs spa, making it an ideal destination for a fun-filled family day out.

Celebrations and Festivals

Malaysia is a vibrant country known for its colourful and lively celebrations, reflecting its multicultural society. These festivities showcase the diverse customs and traditions of the Malay, Chinese, Indian, and indigenous communities. Here are some notable celebrations and festivals in Malaysia:

Hari Raya Aidilfitri

Also known as **Eid al-Fitr**, Hari Raya Aidilfitri marks the end of the Islamic holy month of Ramadan. The celebration spans several days and features special prayers, feasting, and visiting family and friends. Houses are decorated with oil lamps, and children receive gifts or money from elders.

Chinese New Year

Celebrated by the Malaysian Chinese community, the **Lunar New Year** is a 15-day celebration that ushers in the new year according to the Chinese calendar. The festivities include lion and dragon dances, family reunions, feasting, and giving red envelopes containing money to children and unmarried adults.

Deepavali

Also known as **Diwali**, this Hindu festival of lights signifies the triumph of light over darkness and good over evil. Celebrated by the Indian community in Malaysia, Deepavali features the lighting of oil lamps, fireworks, prayers at temples, and feasting on festive foods.

Thaipusam

A significant Hindu festival dedicated to **Lord Murugan**, **Thaipusam** is celebrated by the Tamil community in Malaysia. Devotees participate in a procession, often carrying **kavadis** (large, ornate structures) and piercing their bodies as acts of penance and devotion. The largest Thaipusam celebration takes place at the Batu Caves near Kuala Lumpur.

Hari Merdeka

Malaysia's Independence Day, celebrated on August 31, commemorates the country's independence from British rule in 1957. The celebration includes a national parade, flag-raising ceremonies, and various cultural performances.

Malaysia Day

Celebrated on September 16, **Malaysia Day** marks the formation of Malaysia in 1963 when Malaya, Sabah, Sarawak, and Singapore (which later separated) joined together. The day is observed with patriotic events, cultural performances, and exhibitions.

Christmas

While Malaysia is a predominantly Muslim country, **Christmas** is celebrated by the Christian community and in urban areas. The festivities include church services, family gatherings, and the exchange of gifts. Shopping malls and hotels are often decorated with festive lights and ornaments.

Gawai Dayak

Celebrated by the indigenous people of Sarawak, this harvest festival takes place on June 1 and 2. **Gawai Dayak** features traditional dancing, music, and rituals, as well as the sharing of food and drinks, like the local rice wine called **tuak**.

Hari Raya Haji

Also known as **Eid al-Adha**, this Islamic festival commemorates the willingness of Prophet Ibrahim to sacrifice his son in obedience to God's command. The celebration involves prayers, the distribution of meat to the needy, and visiting family and friends.

Wesak Day

Observed by the Buddhist community, **Wesak Day** celebrates the birth, enlightenment, and passing of **Gautama Buddha**. The festivities include prayers, the release of captive animals, and processions of floats and candles.

11. PRACTICAL TIPS FOR TRAVELLERS AND EXPATS

Safety and Security Tips

Ensuring personal safety and security is important when traveling or living in a foreign country. Here are some practical tips for travellers and expats to stay safe in Malaysia:

Be vigilant in crowded areas

Petty crimes such as pickpocketing, purse-snatching, and theft can occur in busy tourist areas and public transportation hubs. Stay aware of your surroundings and keep your belongings secure at all times.

Don't flaunt valuable items

To avoid attracting unwanted attention, keep expensive jewellery, gadgets, and large sums of cash out of sight when in public.

Be cautious at ATMs

When using an ATM, choose machines in well-lit and busy areas. Be aware of your surroundings, and shield the keypad when entering your PIN.

Observe road safety

Malaysia has different driving habits and road conditions compared to other countries. If you choose to drive, familiarize yourself with local traffic rules and exercise caution. As a pedestrian, use designated crossings and be vigilant when walking near traffic.

Avoid walking alone at night

Especially in poorly lit or unfamiliar areas, it is best to avoid walking alone after dark. If you feel unsafe, trust your instincts and remove yourself from the situation.

Know emergency contacts

Keep a list of emergency contacts, including local police, your home country's embassy or consulate, and personal emergency contacts. In case of emergency, dial 999 for police, ambulance, or fire services in Malaysia.

Secure your home

To protect your residence from break-ins, make sure all doors and windows are secure and consider installing a home security system. Get to know your neighbours, as they can provide valuable support and information in emergencies.

Respect local customs and laws

Familiarize yourself with Malaysia's social customs, taboos, and local laws to avoid accidentally offending anyone or breaking any rules.

Be cautious when accepting offers from strangers

While most Malaysians are warm and hospitable, be wary of potential scams targeting tourists and expats. Exercise caution when accepting offers of assistance or engaging in transactions with strangers.

Stay informed about potential risks

Keep up-to-date with local news and information on potential safety and security risks. By staying informed, you can better prepare for and respond to any situations that may arise.

Healthcare and insurance

Ensuring access to quality healthcare and insurance coverage is essential when traveling or living abroad. Here are some practical tips for travellers and expats in Malaysia regarding healthcare and insurance:

Research the healthcare system

Familiarize yourself with Malaysia's healthcare system, including public and private facilities. Malaysia has a well-developed healthcare system with both public and private facilities available. Private hospitals generally offer a higher standard of care and shorter waiting times but can be more expensive.

Obtain comprehensive travel or expat health insurance

Before your trip, ensure you have adequate health insurance coverage that includes medical treatment, hospitalization, and repatriation. Many travellers and expats opt for international health insurance plans tailored to their specific needs.

Carry your insurance details with you

Always keep your insurance card or a copy of your insurance policy with you, especially when seeking medical treatment. Having this information readily available can help expedite the process and ensure you receive appropriate care.

Know the location of nearby medical facilities

Identify the location of nearby hospitals, clinics, and pharmacies in your area, particularly those with English-speaking staff. In case of an emergency, knowing where to go can save valuable time.

Keep a list of emergency contacts

Have a list of emergency contacts, including your insurance provider's 24-hour helpline, local ambulance services, and your home country's embassy or consulate.

Maintain a well-stocked first aid kit

Keep a first aid kit with essential items such as band-aids, pain relievers, antiseptic wipes, and any prescription medications you may require. This will help you handle minor injuries or illnesses without needing to visit a medical facility.

Get necessary vaccinations

Before traveling to Malaysia, consult your doctor about recommended vaccinations and ensure you are up-to-date with routine immunizations. The Centers for Disease Control and Prevention (CDC) provides guidance on recommended vaccinations for travellers to Malaysia.

Be aware of potential health risks

Familiarize yourself with common health risks in Malaysia, such as dengue fever and foodborne illnesses, and take necessary precautions to minimize your risk.

Practice good hygiene

Maintain good personal hygiene, including washing your hands regularly with soap and water, especially before eating or preparing food. This can help prevent the spread of illness and infections.

Maintain a healthy lifestyle

While living in Malaysia, maintain a balanced diet, exercise regularly, and get enough sleep to support your overall health and well-being.

12. OVERCOMING STEREOTYPES AND PREJUDICES

Common Misconceptions and Stereotypes

Malaysia is a diverse and multicultural country, but like any nation, it is subject to misconceptions and stereotypes. Here are some common misconceptions and stereotypes about Malaysia that should be debunked:

Malaysia is an Islamic country

While Islam is the official religion and the majority of Malaysians are Muslim, the country is not an Islamic state. Malaysia has a secular constitution and recognizes the freedom of religion, with significant populations of Buddhists, Christians, Hindus, and followers of other faiths.

Malaysia is unsafe

Malaysia is generally considered a safe country for travellers and expats. However, as in any country, petty crime and other safety risks exist. Visitors and residents should remain vigilant and follow safety precautions, but Malaysia's overall safety situation should not be exaggerated.

All Malaysians speak Malay

While Malay is the official language and spoken by the majority, Malaysia's linguistic landscape is diverse. Many Malaysians are bilingual or multilingual, speaking languages such as English, Mandarin, Tamil, and various indigenous languages.

Malaysia is underdeveloped

Malaysia is often mistakenly considered a developing or underdeveloped country. In reality, it is an upper-middle-income nation with a rapidly growing economy and a high Human Development Index. The country has modern infrastructure, a high standard of living, and well-developed healthcare and education systems.

Malaysia's climate is always hot and humid

While Malaysia does have a tropical climate, the weather can vary depending on the region and elevation. Coastal areas tend to be hot and humid, while the highlands offer cooler temperatures and more temperate conditions.

Malaysia is synonymous with Kuala Lumpur

While Kuala Lumpur is Malaysia's capital and largest city, the country has much more to offer. Malaysia boasts diverse landscapes, including pristine beaches, lush rainforests, and charming colonial towns. It is also home to a rich cultural tapestry of Malay, Chinese, Indian, and indigenous influences.

Malaysian food is all spicy

Although many Malaysian dishes are known for their rich, spicy flavours, the cuisine is diverse and caters to a wide range of palates. Malaysian food incorporates various culinary traditions, including Malay, Chinese, Indian, and Nyonya, offering a multitude of flavours and textures.

Malaysians are conservative and unwelcoming

While it is true that some Malaysians hold conservative values, particularly in rural areas, the majority of people are warm, friendly, and welcoming towards foreigners. Respect for local customs and traditions is essential, but most Malaysians are open to cultural exchange and eager to share their way of life with visitors.

Strategies for overcoming biases and promoting understanding

As with any foreign country, it's important to approach a different culture with an open mind and a willingness to learn about its culture and people. Here are some strategies for overcoming biases and promoting understanding:

Learn about the culture and history

Learn about the culture and history before visiting or living in the country. This can help you gain a better understanding of the customs, traditions, and beliefs of its people.

Engage with the local community

Engage with the local community to learn about their daily lives, customs, and traditions. This can help you develop a deeper appreciation and understanding of their culture.

Avoid stereotypes and assumptions

Avoid making assumptions or generalizations about the people or culture. Recognize that diversity exists within the country and that each individual has their own unique experiences and perspectives.

Be respectful and open-minded

Be respectful and open-minded when interacting with locals. Show interest in their culture and traditions and avoid imposing your own beliefs or values.

Learn the language

Learn some basic phrases to help you communicate with the local community. This can help you build rapport and establish a deeper connection with the people.

Participate in cultural activities

Participate in cultural activities such as festivals and ceremonies to learn more about the customs and traditions of the local community. This can also help you build relationships and connect with others.

Seek out diverse perspectives

Seek out diverse perspectives on the country and its culture, including those of different ethnic groups and social classes. This can help you gain a more nuanced and comprehensive understanding of the country and its people.

13. BUILDING CROSS-CULTURAL RELATIONSHIPS

Effective Communication and Conflict Resolution

Effective communication and conflict resolution are key components of building cross-cultural relationships. Here are some tips for expats on effective communication and conflict resolution:

Learn the language

Learning some basic phrases can help you communicate more effectively with the local community. This can help you establish rapport and build relationships with locals.

Be aware of nonverbal cues

Be aware of nonverbal cues such as body language and tone of voice, which can vary depending on the culture. Locals may use indirect communication and nonverbal cues to express their thoughts and feelings, so it's important to be sensitive to these cues.

Listen actively

Active listening is an important part of effective communication. Take the time to listen to the perspectives and concerns of locals and show that you understand and value their opinions.

Be respectful

Be respectful of the culture and traditions. Show interest and respect for their beliefs and customs and avoid imposing your own values or beliefs.

Avoid confrontation

Locals may avoid confrontation or direct conflict, preferring instead to use indirect communication and negotiation. Be mindful of this and avoid being confrontational in your communication style.

Seek to understand

Seek to understand the perspective and context in any conflict or disagreement. This can help you find common ground and work towards a mutually acceptable solution.

Be patient

Building cross-cultural relationships takes time and patience. Be patient in your communication and conflict resolution and be willing to compromise and find creative solutions.

Adapting to cultural differences

Adapting to cultural differences is an important part of living as an expat. Here are some tips for expats on how to adapt to cultural differences:

Learn about the culture

Learn about the culture and customs before you arrive. This can help you understand the social norms, values, and beliefs.

Respect local customs

Respect local customs and traditions, even if they are different from what you are used to. Show interest in the culture and be willing to learn and adapt.

Develop relationships

Develop relationships with locals, whether it's with colleagues, neighbours, or friends. This can help you gain a better understanding of the culture and develop a support network.

Learn the language

Learning some basic phrases can help you communicate more effectively with nationals and show that you respect their culture.

Be patient

Be patient and understanding of cultural differences. Locals may have a different sense of time, communication style, and decision-making process than what you are used to.

Be flexible

Be flexible and adaptable in your approach to work and socializing. Locals may have different work and social customs, so be willing to adjust your expectations and approach.

Embrace new experiences

Embrace new experiences and try new things, such as trying local food, attending cultural events, or visiting new places. This can help you appreciate and enjoy the unique aspects of the culture.

Developing empathy and cultural intelligence

Developing empathy and cultural intelligence is essential for fostering meaningful cross-cultural relationships, both personally and professionally. In this chapter, we will discuss strategies and tips for cultivating empathy and cultural intelligence to better connect with people from different backgrounds.

Educate yourself about different cultures.

Invest time in learning about the values, customs, and traditions of various cultures, especially those you frequently interact with. Understanding cultural nuances can help you appreciate their perspectives and anticipate potential communication challenges.

Engage in active listening.

Make a conscious effort to listen attentively to others, without interrupting or imposing your own opinions. Active listening can help you gain deeper insights into their experiences, feelings, and perspectives, which is crucial for developing empathy.

Practice perspective-taking.

Put yourself in the shoes of others and try to understand their thoughts, emotions, and experiences from their point of view. This can help you appreciate the challenges they face and foster empathy and understanding.

Develop emotional intelligence.

Emotional intelligence refers to the ability to recognize, understand, and manage your own emotions and the emotions of others. Enhancing your emotional intelligence can help you better understand the emotional underpinnings of cross-cultural interactions and respond more empathetically.

Be curious and open-minded.

Approach cultural differences with curiosity and an open mind. Ask questions and seek to learn more about the experiences and perspectives of others, without judgment or preconceived notions.

Observe and reflect on cultural interactions.

Pay close attention to how you and others respond to cultural differences in various contexts. Reflect on these interactions to identify areas where you can improve your empathy and cultural intelligence.

Seek diverse experiences and relationships.

Expose yourself to diverse experiences and relationships by interacting with people from different cultural backgrounds. These experiences can help you develop a broader understanding of the world and enhance your empathy and cultural intelligence.

Foster a growth mindset.

Embrace a growth mindset, which involves viewing challenges as opportunities for learning and growth. This mindset can help you approach cultural differences with a willingness to learn and adapt, rather than feeling threatened or overwhelmed.

Participate in cultural training and workshops.

Consider attending workshops or participating in cultural training programs to enhance your understanding of different cultures and develop your empathy and cultural intelligence.

Continuously learn and adapt.

Recognize that developing empathy and cultural intelligence is an ongoing process that requires continuous learning, reflection, and adaptation. Stay committed to personal growth and be open to feedback and new experiences.

14. CASE STUDIES AND REAL LIFE EXAMPLES

Stories and anecdotes illustrating cultural challenges and successes

Cross-cultural communication challenge:

An American expat was working on a project in Malaysia and had to collaborate with a team of local Malaysian employees. The American was used to a direct communication style and often provided constructive criticism to the team members. However, they soon noticed that the Malaysian team members were becoming less responsive and seemed to be avoiding interactions with the expat.

Upon discussing the issue with a local friend, the American learned that Malaysians generally prefer a more indirect communication style, especially when discussing sensitive topics or providing feedback. The direct approach of the American expat was perceived as confrontational and disrespectful. To remedy the situation, the expat adopted a more indirect communication style, using phrases like "It might be helpful to consider…" instead of directly pointing out issues. This change in approach helped improve communication and collaboration with the Malaysian team members.

Overcoming cultural differences in social norms:

A British couple moved to Malaysia for work and rented an apartment in a predominantly Muslim neighbourhood. They soon discovered that their Muslim neighbours would sometimes leave their shoes outside their homes when entering. Wanting to respect the local customs, the British couple began doing the same.

One day, the couple invited their neighbours over for a meal. Although they served halal food and avoided alcohol, they noticed that their guests seemed uneasy. Upon asking if something was wrong, they learned that their guests were not comfortable sitting on the same chairs that the couple had used while wearing their outdoor clothes. The couple quickly understood their mistake, and they brought out cushions for their guests to sit on, which made them more comfortable. The experience taught the couple about the importance of understanding local customs and adapting to them.

A successful multicultural team:

A multinational corporation opened a new branch in Malaysia, bringing together employees from diverse backgrounds, including Malays, Chinese Malaysians, Indian Malaysians, and expats from various countries. Initially, there were communication issues and cultural misunderstandings among team members, affecting the overall productivity.

To address these issues, the company organized a series of team-building exercises and cultural awareness workshops. These activities helped the employees learn more about each other's cultures, work styles, and communication preferences. As a result, they began to appreciate their differences and leverage their diverse skills and perspectives to create a more cohesive and successful team.

Navigating cultural differences in business etiquette:

A European business executive travelled to Malaysia for a series of important meetings with potential partners. Upon arrival, they were greeted with a traditional Malaysian handshake, which involved touching their counterpart's hand, then placing their hand over their heart. Although it felt unusual to the executive, they quickly learned to reciprocate the gesture, demonstrating respect for their hosts' customs.

During meetings, the executive noticed that Malaysian colleagues would often nod their head and say "yes" when listening, even if they did not necessarily agree with the point being made. The executive realized that this was a sign of active listening and politeness, rather than an indication of agreement. By adapting to these cultural nuances, the executive was able to build trust and rapport with their Malaysian counterparts, ultimately leading to successful business negotiations.

Lessons learned and best practices

The case studies and examples illustrate the importance of cultural awareness and adaptation when visiting or living in a foreign culture. Here are some lessons learned and best practices for navigating cultural challenges and embracing local customs:

Learn about the culture and customs

Before traveling to or living in there, take the time to research and understand the country's history, culture, traditions, and customs. This knowledge will help you avoid misunderstandings, build relationships, and appreciate the richness of the culture.

Be open-minded and adaptable

Recognize that cultural norms and practices may differ from what you're used to. Be willing to adapt your behaviour and communication style to show respect and appreciation for the local culture.

Practice patience and humility

When faced with cultural differences or challenges, remain patient and humble. Be willing to learn from others and ask for help or guidance when needed.

Develop language skills

Even basic knowledge of the language can help you connect with locals, navigate daily life, and show respect for the culture. Practice speaking, listening, and reading to enhance your communication skills and overall experience.

Observe and learn from locals

Pay attention to how locals interact, communicate, and behave in various situations. Learning from observation can provide valuable insights into cultural norms and expectations.

Show respect for religious customs and traditions

Be aware of local customs and etiquette when visiting religious sites, such as temples. Dress modestly, remove your shoes, and follow any specific guidelines provided.

Be aware of nonverbal communication

Most cultures place great importance on nonverbal cues, such as facial expressions, body language, and tone of voice. Be attentive to these cues and learn to interpret them accurately to avoid misunderstandings.

Choose ethical and responsible tourism options

Support local communities and protect the environment by choosing sustainable and responsible travel experiences. Be mindful of your impact on the local culture, environment, and economy.

Build relationships

Invest time and effort in building relationships with people, whether they are colleagues, neighbours, or friends. Developing strong connections can lead to a deeper understanding of the culture and a more fulfilling experience.

Reflect on your experiences

Take the time to reflect on your experiences, challenges, and successes. Consider what you have learned and how you can continue to grow and adapt to different cultural contexts.

Resources and Further Reading

Books, articles, and websites for further exploration

Books:

- "A Short History of Malaysia: Linking East and West" by Virginia Matheson Hooker
- "The Malay Dilemma" by Mahathir Mohamad
- "Malaysia: A Pictorial History 1400-2004" by Wendy Khadijah Moore
- "Malaysia: Recipes from a Family Kitchen" by Ping Coombes

- "CultureShock! Malaysia: A Survival Guide to Customs and Etiquette" by Heidi Munan

<u>Articles:</u>

- "Understanding Malaysian Culture" by N. Tarling - Asian Studies Review, Volume 22, 1998 - Issue 3
- "Multiculturalism in Malaysia: Individual Harmony, Group Tension" by Maznah Mohamad - Rajaratnam School of International Studies, 2010
- "The Impact of Culture on Tourism in Malaysia" by Fatemeh Khozaei, Zeinab Khozaei - Procedia - Social and Behavioral Sciences, Volume 42, 2012"10

<u>Websites:</u>

- Malaysian Insider (https://www.malaysianow.com/) - A news website covering Malaysian politics, society, and culture.
- National Museum of Malaysia (http://www.muziumnegara.gov.my/) - The official website of the National Museum of Malaysia, offering information about Malaysian history, art, and culture.
- Expat.com Malaysia (https://www.expat.com/en/destination/asia/malaysia/) - A community-driven website with forums, articles, and resources for expats living in Malaysia.
- Lonely Planet Malaysia (https://www.lonelyplanet.com/malaysia) - A travel guide for Malaysia, including information on cultural attractions, history, and customs.

Language learning resources and cultural organisations

<u>Language Learning Resources:</u>

- Duolingo (https://www.duolingo.com/course/ms/en/Learn-Malay) - A popular free language learning platform offering lessons in Malay.
- Memrise (https://www.memrise.com/courses/english/malay/) - Another popular language learning platform with various courses in Malay, focusing on vocabulary and phrases.
- Transparent Language (https://www.transparent.com/learn-malay/) - Offers online courses in Malay, including audio lessons, flashcards, and quizzes.
- Learn Malay Online (https://www.learnmalayonline.com/) - Offers free online resources, lessons, and quizzes for learning Malay.
- iTalki (https://www.italki.com/) - A platform that connects language learners with native speakers for one-on-one lessons, including Malay tutors.

<u>Cultural Organizations:</u>

- The Malaysian Cultural Organization (MCO) (http://www.mculture.org/) - A non-profit organization dedicated to promoting Malaysian culture, arts, and heritage.
- The National Department for Culture and Arts Malaysia (JKKN) (https://www.jkkn.gov.my/) - A government agency responsible for promoting and preserving Malaysian culture, arts, and heritage.
- Malaysian Heritage and History Club (MHHC) (https://www.facebook.com/malaysianheritageandhistory/) - A club that organizes events, talks, and tours to promote awareness and appreciation of Malaysian history and heritage.
- The Malaysia Society (https://www.malaysiasociety.org/) - A UK-based organization that aims to promote understanding and friendship between the people of Malaysia and the United Kingdom through cultural, educational, and social activities.
- The Malaysian-American Society (MAS) (https://www.malaysian-american.org/) - A US-based organization that aims to foster cultural exchange, friendship, and understanding between Malaysians and Americans.

www.ingramcontent.com/pod-product-compliance
Lightning Source LLC
Chambersburg PA
CBHW070456220526
45466CB00004B/1854